WANDERING IN JAPAN
THE SPIRIT OF TOKYO, KYOTO AND BEYOND

Other Wanderland Writers Anthologies

WANDERING IN JAPAN
THE SPIRIT OF TOKYO, KYOTO AND BEYOND

Edited by
Linda Watanabe McFerrin and
Laurie McAndish King

Wanderland Writers
Oakland, California

For permission to print essays in this volume, grateful acknowledgement is made to
the holders of copyright named on pages 187-195.

Photographs are in public domain, except as noted:
Front cover © Jim Shubin
Back cover © Lowry McFerrin (editors), Jim Shubin
Pages 36, 56, 186 © Jim Shubin
Pages 54, 178 © Laurie McAndish King
Pages 82, 114, 134 © Linda Watanabe McFerrin
Page 92 © Jim Shubin (pizza)/Utamaro Kitagawa (woodcut from 1796)
Page 102 © Olga Aniven/Shutterstock
Pages 108, 142 © Tania Amochaev Romanov
Page 172 © Lowry McFerrin

Cover design, interior design and map by Jim Shubin,
www.bookalchemist.net

CATALOGING DATA:
Wandering in Japan: The Spirit of Tokyo, Kyoto and Beyond
Edited by Linda Watanabe McFerrin and Laurie McAndish King

ISBN: 978-1-7374502-8-3
First printing 2022
Printed in the United States of America

For Masakatsu "Katsu" Miyata (1950-2021)

beloved friend and world traveler

Special thanks to Marian Goldberg, whose knowledge, direction and patience helped make this book a reality.

Welcome to Japan

CONTENTS

JAPAN

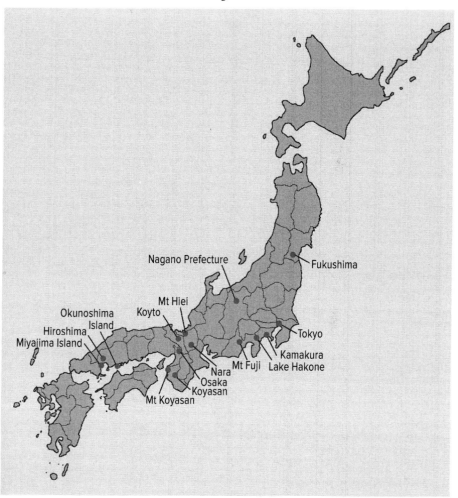

Nagano Prefecture

Fukushima

Mt Hiei

Koyto

Okunoshima
Island

Hiroshima
Miyajima Island

Tokyo

Kamakura
Mt Fuji   Lake Hakone

Nara
Osaka
Koyasan

Mt Koyasan

INTRODUCTION

For many, traveling to Japan is like landing on another planet. This island nation with a rich, 30,000-year cultural and spiritual history never fails to fascinate, intrigue and sometimes befuddle visitors. When you journey to Japan, you know you have arrived in a place where the line between this reality and the next disappears, where the good can be found in the bad and what's bizarre, exotic and unexpected can, in a moment, become quite ordinary and mundane. In this kaleidoscope of a world, it is all too easy to disappear down a rabbit hole—or should we say, foxhole—of mind, body and spirit.

The writers sharing their stories in this collection have discovered just that. From encounters with ancestors, ghosts, demons and kind spirit animals; from *kaieseki* to *chindogu* to *kawaii* culture; from quiet shrines to dark city streets to mystifying mountain monasteries; our contributors crisscrossed this Land of the Rising Sun, exploring a terrain that refracts and reflects our staid understanding of self.

Demanding Buddhas, walking vacuum cleaners, beckoning pizzas, and samurai who refuse to die are among the characters encountered by our writers, as are talking toilets, waving cats and magical foxes. Within these pages you will climb Mount Fuji, experience a religious initiation and discover the secrets of Kobe beef. You will learn about unique aspects of Japanese family dynamics and uncover the riddle of a Buddha that is "both high and low." You will even share breakfast with one of the founders of Sony.

And that is only a sampling of what you will encounter. We hope you will visit Japan. Here first, and then on your own journey to Tokyo, Kyoto and beyond.

—*Linda Watanabe McFerrin and Laurie McAndish King*
Oakland, California and Novato, California

Foreword

I wasn't planning to fall in love with Japan.

I was approaching the end of a graduate school program in creative writing and didn't know what to do with my life. I realized that I knew next to nothing about Asia, and a one-year post-undergraduate stay in France and Greece had taught me that living in a foreign country was the best way to learn about it, so I decided to apply for a Princeton-in-Asia fellowship. I would return to the classroom of the world!

Of all the Asian countries where fellowships were offered, Japan seemed the most modern and so probably the easiest one to live in, so I applied there. Though I knew virtually nothing about the country, I was awarded a fellowship to teach at International Christian University in a suburb of Tokyo—and that's when everything changed.

For the first half-year of my two-year fellowship, I felt exceedingly disoriented. Nothing made sense. I couldn't read the signs in the streets or the shops, and I couldn't read the signs in the people either. I didn't understand the cultural concepts or social rules; everything felt foreign.

Then one morning almost exactly six months after I arrived, I woke up and it was as if all the pieces of the puzzle had clicked into place. Suddenly everything made sense.

In retrospect, I realize that I had finally surrendered. I had given myself up to Japan rather than trying to impose my American notions of coherence and order on it. From that moment on, I began to notice all the things I had missed: the kindness, attentiveness, and thoughtfulness of the people, the exquisite sense of aesthetics in everything from the humblest package to the most expansive garden, the sense of pride, honesty, and honor in everyday life, the quality of the craftsmanship, the beauty of the countryside, the reverence for nature, the embrace of stillness and silence, the celebration of life's fleeting beauty.

I fell in love with the country and the culture. And before long I fell in love with a Japanese woman as well, and this opened ever deeper layers of mystery and magic.

That was 45 years ago, and Japan has been intertwined with my life ever since. Its riches remain inexhaustible and its depths unfathomable, but as the years have aged us, I find myself appreciating the country more and more.

Now, wherever I am, I am in Japan, and Japan is in me.

Every day is like a spring shower of cherry blossoms—exquisitely short-lived, incomparably beautiful, whispering its return even as it swirls to the ground. Every year is like a Hagi tea bowl, cradled by countless hands, seasoned by a succession of soulful sighs, textured and sheened by the wisdom of time. Every life is like the single sprig arranged in the tea room *tokonoma*, gathering all the world into itself, holding everything in its infinite space, suspending each moment in its everlasting grace.

—*Don George*
Piedmont, California

"Mount Fuji" woodblock print by Katsushika Hokusai

FUJI FOOL

Mary Brent Cantarutti

Everyone should climb Mount Fuji once;
he who climbs it twice is a fool.

—Japanese proverb

It was 2:30 in the morning; the crescent moon had nodded away at the eighth station on Fuji-san, Japan's most famous peak. Icy daggers of horizontal rain pelted us unmercifully. I shivered against my will, trapped inside a freezing cocoon of soggy high-tech fiber, and prayed for deliverance.

Thanks to my son, Perry, an airline employee living in Tokyo, the storybook images of Japan were coming to life on this trip: lacy red maples, patterns raked in white sand, faces captured in ageless stone. Mount Fuji cast its own spell, a mystical peak seemingly rising from nowhere, glimpsed from the window of a plane or speeding *Shinkansen*.

It was mid-July when Perry wrote that he and a small group of friends were planning to climb Mount Fuji in August. "Want to

1

join us?" he asked. His brother, Jeffrey, was copied on the email.

The flight from San Francisco to Narita Airport went like clockwork. Jeffrey and I toasted our good fortune. Beyond a losing nine-hour battle with the sun, jet lag and a sixteen-hour time difference, there was nothing to cloud my fantasy of climbing Mount Fuji: A sea of polite Japanese pilgrims ascend a defined path lit by a full moon or occasional lantern, a ubiquitous flag in the lead. In the dead of night, we melt into the line—together we watch the sunrise at the summit.

Friday noon the following day, five of us met to finalize plans. Shinjuku Station, 7:30 that evening, was the rendezvous point. Perry's friend, Melissa, reminded us to bring sunscreen. It would be quite warm at the summit. A quick walk around the rim, a leisurely descent, and we should be back in Tokyo by noon on Saturday.

We stepped out of the cab at Shinjuku Station laden with bottled water, Clif Bars, trail mix, M&M's, flashlights, hats, gloves and scarves. Sticky sweat condensed in secret pools under my layers of fleece. Melissa spotted Nazomi, her Japanese friend, and Tim Liu, the sixth climber, among the swirling masses of commuters. We exchanged polite introductions.

The chartered bus was packed; latecomers claimed fold-out seats in the aisle. Most of the passengers were Japanese. Given the individual attire—everything from jeans, shorts and lightweight jackets to sandals and heavy-duty hiking gear—it was hard to believe we were all bound for the same rising sun.

Dusk faded to inky blackness; I could hear lazy rain falling against small glass panes. The bus snaked higher and higher. Two and a half hours later, 10:00 p.m. at the fifth station, we finally set foot on Mount Fuji.

Welcoming light radiated from a nearby store. Inside we discovered an amazing assortment of kitsch, smelly plastic raingear and even bottled oxygen. Walking sticks, adorned with brightly colored streamers and three silver bells, were a must. We'd start out with a jingle and have a distinctive mark burned into the sticks—for a price—at each of the five stations along the way.

Everyone on the bus had disappeared into the starless, drizzly night. We followed a wide smooth path that led to huge cobblestones. Out of nowhere rose the sacred mountain—an expression of the gods—sharp, jagged, random, steep, steeper. Save for an occasional white arrow sprayed on a rock, there were no signs anywhere. None, mind you, and it was dark; darker than I ever remembered.

One step at a time ran through my mind like a survival mantra. There was nothing but me, us, the mountain—and Jeffrey's slippery footsteps to follow. The ascent between the sixth and seventh stations was particularly arduous. We stopped to catch our breath and admire the clearing sky and bright sprinkling of stars. The summit was suddenly a real promise.

Melissa and Perry were waiting for us at the eighth station, huddled in front of a dark wooden hut. It was 2:30 a.m. The heavens were suddenly wailing, hiking conditions were turning dangerous-to-impossible, and the temperature was plummeting. We decided to seek a few hours of refuge within the hut.

Nazomi and the kimono-clad man standing sentry conversed in Japanese. The "rack rate," 5,000 yen or $50 a night, was nonnegotiable. We entered, grateful for the wet yen buried in our pockets, and followed Nazomi's instructions. Our dripping outerwear, including boots, was shed on the spot and placed inside the large plastic bag handed to each of us. I longingly eyed the pot of tea brewing on the low stove; nothing was offered. We followed the white kimono, tiptoeing down dimly lit corridors until we reached our shared resting place: a tiny section of a long wooden slab—the lower of two stacked platforms covered with tattered mats.

Loud snores confirmed that we were not alone. Stripped down to damp tights and a long sleeve T-shirt, I squeezed between my two sons. For the first time I heard the rain, a crescendo of angry ice pulsing on the tin roof. I finally fell into a fitful sleep, one question running through my mind: *How are we going to get off this mountain?*

At 5:30 we were jolted awake by sudden glaring light and a strident male voice barking out orders in Japanese. Sleepy climbers spilled from the stacks of unforgiving wood like resurrected sardines.

"What's happening, Nazomi, what's he saying?" Perry inquired groggily.

"'Get up, get up, the tour is leaving.' That's what he said," Nazomi replied, adding that we could stay in the hut until 7:00. I clung to the threadbare blanket, praying that the deluge would cease. Our spokesperson was up at 6:45, dressed in wet layers salvaged from her plastic bag, quietly eating the snacks from her backpack. Grumbling, we followed her stoic lead.

A quick stop at the fetid outdoor latrine—50 yen collected at the entrance—and we were on the downside of the mountain. The porous red earth offered up hunks of itself in swelling fits and starts. Rain, rain, rain. And there were the Japanese pilgrims of my fantasy—except they were like packs of silent refugees, resolutely marching in a straight line, soggy umbrellas in the lead.

My walking stick, streaked with red dye from the streamers, was no match for the heaving mountain. I stuck to the center of the

4

collapsing path, slipping, sliding all the way. I fell once, fell twice.
"Mom, grab my arm. We're going to get off this mountain." It
was Jeffrey.

Arm in arm, we careened down Mount Fuji, skipping over
rivulets of mud, passing first aid stations and donkey-drawn rescue
carts. The fifth station seemed like a war zone. Men shouted orders
through megaphones; people scurried around circled buses. We
didn't understand one spoken word. Cold, soaked to the bone, I
couldn't stop shaking. Jeffrey folded me into his arms, sharing the
warmth of his body and down jacket while we waited for the
others.

Thanks to Nazomi, we learned that roads were closed due to
flash floods. In fact, the last bus was leaving the fifth station in
minutes. Threads of civility were lost as we shoved our way onto
the jam-packed bus, only to be dropped off after several miles, left
to fend for ourselves in a countryside dotted with swollen rice
fields.

Guess who charted the long course back to Tokyo, guiding us
on and off rural buses and trains? Nazomi left us at Shinjuku
Station, almost exactly twenty-four hours after our original
departure. I bowed slightly and said, "Thanks," as she slipped away.

Only fools. I could hear the mountain whispering over and over
again: *Only fools climb Mount Fuji twice.* For me, once was enough.

Antique obake image from Tosa Province (now Kōchi Prefecture)

SPOOKY, SPOOKY TOKYO

Linda Watanabe McFerrin

A shadow world gloated between the skinny fingers of lamplight, pointing a quavering path through the bicycle-cluttered back streets that twist through the Shitamachi, one of the oldest portions of Tokyo. If it weren't for my landlord, Mr. Sawa, I'd be lost. He was leading me on a night tour through the labyrinthine, old-style neighborhood that surrounds his inn, or *ryokan*, and his tour was creeping me out.

Earlier in the day, with the sunlight streaming, dreamy and creamy, over stone temple walls, I had visited the umbrella shops, bookstores, bakeries, bathhouses, tatami makers, noodle shops, florists and shrines indicated on the hand-drawn, hand-lettered map Mr. Sawa had given me. This was old Tokyo, a place in the northeastern section of the metropolis where the wooden, two-story houses and shops—spared the earthquakes, fires and bombs that ravaged the rest of the city—hearken back to an ancient era. I had ice-cold soba noodles for lunch, meditated at a Shinto shrine and strolled along overgrown, leaf-scattered paths at Yanaka Cemetery, weaving my way in and out amid the headstones. It seemed such a pleasant and non-threatening place. In Japan the cemeteries are almost like parks. The cheerful home of one's ancestors, families gather and picnic within them. But late at night, with the click-click of Mr. Sawa's wooden sandals, or geta, ticking through the darkness far ahead of me, I was not exactly at ease.

Sometimes Tokyo spooks me. As a child, I lived with my grandmother in the city's racy Roppongi district—a kid from the U.S. in the clutches of an other-worldly land. Public baths, attack toilets, dogs dressed in two-piece plaid suits—these are cultural oddities from which anyone can recover. But the footless, phosphorescent *obake*—women who died with a grudge; the angry demons, or *oni*, with their ruby-red eyes; and the faceless ghost with no eyes, nose, or mouth who walks Akasaka road, weeping; played long-term mental mischief on me. I've since found that the Japanese are quite comfortable with the supernatural. Their phantoms and wraiths are the repositories for unspoken feelings. They absorb and act out the stresses and fears that might upset public balance; they fulfill a significant purpose. So, it's only natural that the Japanese are actually fond of their specters and make sure there's a place for them in their otherwise smiling, happy, "Hello-Kitty" world.

In the Ginza, one of the premier shopping areas in Tokyo quite close to the center of town, for example, the mood gets altogether creepy around the Kabuki-za. With its enormous lanterns and shadowy eaves this theater draws crowds daily with its canon of traditional plays. Best to book a ticket to watch as the all-male cast is tormented, murdered, grossly transformed and provoked to suicide in an explosion of color and chaos as spirits reach out from beyond the grave to test and to tempt them. Translation tapes are available for the hauntingly musical language. The plays last for hours, but you can come and go between acts, and you'll have plenty of company in the cramped seats lined up, row upon row, in the darkness.

Not far from the Kabuki-za, if one continues south along Harumi-dori, Tsukiji Fish Market, the largest municipal market in Japan, stood for centuries. One third of all the fish eaten in Japan moved through Tsukiji. To unfamiliar eyes, the tuna auction, which generally began at around 5 a.m., seemed as obscure and mysterious as an ancient druidical rite. The tuna was frozen to kill parasites and germs, and an ectoplasmic fog emanated from the cadavers as the auctioneers did their work. Other unusual forms of sea life, kept alive in tubs of running water, made the experience seem like an alien encounter. In this version, though, the people were eating the aliens.

Shinjuku at night can also be an eerie affair. Even after the Ginza, the fast-paced Shinjuku district with its skyscrapers and towers can come as a bit of a shock. Entire cities exist within the walls of some of its forty- and fifty-story edifices. North and west of the city's center, at the juncture of what were once Tokyo's most important roads, Shinjuku Station is easily the busiest station in Tokyo. More than three million people pass through it each day, and plenty of them seem to stay for the night. Just north of Yasukuni-dori and east of Seibu Shinjuku Station is Kabuki-cho, a red-light district peppered with massage parlors, strip clubs, peep shows and love hotels. Tiny bars, or *nomiya*, in the Golden Gai serve locals in "members' clubs" that welcome everyone from salarymen to gangsters, but rarely the stranger in town. It seems so much more sensible to look down on the lurid scene from the wholesome ambiance of the

40th floor Japanese restaurant, Kozue, in the Park Hyatt Tokyo. Perched high in the heavens with a clear view of Mount Fuji, one feels safe from all shady and unsavory apparitions. The only spirits anyone is likely encounter will be the fine wines and sake that accompany a kaiseki-style meal or the graceful essence of the antique earthenware pottery that often adorns the tables.

Another chilling venue, if one approaches from the Asakusa subway station by way of the Kaminari-mon (Thunder Gate) is Asakusa Kannon Temple, also known as Sensoji Temple. Situated not far from the banks of the Sumida River that forms Tokyo's eastern boundary in the district of Asakusa, it is also a part of the ancient downtown. At the Thunder Gate two frightening protector deities—Fujin, the god of wind, and Raijin, the god of thunder—guard the entrance. Behind these terrifying gods stretches the carnival of kiosks and shops known as Nakamise-dori where one finds scary Noh masks, demon-head key rings, antique armor, plastic samurai swords, kamikaze headbands, T-shirts and trinkets. If one survives this gaudy gauntlet with wits and wallet intact, one can climb the temple steps, toss a coin in the wooden offertory box, clap hands together and catch the attention of the deity for a few quiet seconds. Or invest in a look at the future. A dollar will purchase a fortune to hang up near the door of the temple. If the fortune is bad, you can buy another, and another, until you are satisfied.

If you're hedging your bets, it's a good idea, before you do this, to cleanse yourself with the incense that smokes just inside the Kanando Hozomon Gate at the base of the temple steps. Over 30 million people visit every year to pray or bathe in the healing smoke of this incense. Unlike Buddhist temples, Shinto shrines prohibit the use of incense as impure and displeasing to the older gods, but at every Buddhist temple cheap incense is burning to drive away goblins and the evil powers that preside over a pantheon of diseases. Interestingly, incense was formerly used to summon spirits as well as to banish them. It seems smoke is a language understood by the dead.

Oh, yes, the dead. The best time to encounter them in Tokyo is during O'Bon. On the thirteenth day of the seventh month of the year, the great Festival of the Dead commences. For three days in July, the living give the dead a spirited welcome. Lanterns are hung to guide ghosts to their homes. Families set food out on the *shoryodana*, or shelf of souls, under moonlight. Incense rises, paper obake hang and turn in the wind, ivory-faced devils glower, and chants, prayers and invocations litter the air with expectation and remorse.

Of course, that night as I walked through the dimly lit streets with Mr. Sawa, I knew it was coming. As I trudged along behind him on our way to his favorite watering hole, he decided to tell me a story. It seemed we were on the very road that a certain high-ranking maiden by the name of Tsuyu travels every night to meet a young samurai who resided near Nezu. She carries a peony lantern and is always accompanied by her loyal maidservant, O-Yoné. Tsuyu and the samurai fell in love at first sight, but he never called on her again. Tsuyu pined away and died. Today, she can be found in Yanaka-no-Sasaki at the temple of Shin-Banzui-In. In the cemetery, right where her grave should be, is the grave of a Buddhist nun. Next to this grave is the grave of a Nezu merchant named Kichibei. It is in this grave that Hagiwara Shizaburo, the samurai with whom Tsuyu fell in love, is supposed to lie. But apparently the information is wrong, or Tsuyu doesn't know this, because every night she returns to the samurai's Nezu home. *Kara-*

kon, kara-kon—the sound of her geta echoing over the darkened streets lets the neighborhood know she is passing.

Listening to Sawa-san's geta beat their redundant tattoo on the pavement, I shuddered. It felt like the door between two worlds had opened. Instead, it was the pub door that opened, and I felt the sudden flush of warmth and laughter. Grateful for the camaraderie, I settled down to my usual struggle with unusual appetizers and the mysteries of Japanese conversation. Everyone knows that the best protection from ghosts is good company. I was glad, most of all, that my landlord was walking me home.

The omnipresent good fortune kitty (maneki-neko)

Chindogu and the Origin of the Selfie Stick

Laurie McAndish King

Three Tenets of Chindogu (Selected):

1. Chindogu must be (almost) completely useless
3. Inherent in every chindogu is the spirit of anarchy
5. Chindogu are not for sale

—Kenji Kawakama

Japan—the birthplace of karaoke, pachinko parlors and love hotels, not to mention walking ice-cream cones and talking toilets—intrigued me with its endless peculiarities. I've been captivated by strange things for as long as I can remember because, well ... I grew up in a strange family. Mom, a city girl who moved to Dad's hometown—population 4,151—shortly after they married, was always as out-of-place as a Unitarian in catechism class. She wore her hair in a blunt-cut bob when the other moms were doing beehives. She fed our family rich Indian curries, Italian chicken cacciatore, spicy Mexican tacos and cardamom-laced halvah while my friends ate meat and potatoes. She traveled widely, helped a

Laotian refugee family learn English and decorated our home with indigenous masks, prayer bells, colorful tapestries, wood carvings and other exotica that must, now that I think back on it, have seemed downright bizarre to the neighbors.

Dad loved tinkering and inventing things. He built a good-sized telescope, taught himself computer coding back in the 1980s, and created a detailed scale map of the local cemetery, providing the first formal documentation of the final resting places of thousands of the late citizens of Monroe County, Iowa. His desk was cluttered with a microscope and slides, Mason jars filled with samples of pond water in varying stages of green stagnation, and stacks of notebooks for recording his observations of protozoa. He worked for decades as a senior UFO investigator, checking out sightings—and even apparent encounters—all across the midwestern states. That put him pretty much at the top of the weirdness pyramid.

So, it's no wonder that on my first visit to Japan I was obsessed—although a bit overwhelmed—by its relentless eccentricity. In Kyoto, my first stop, I observed women roaming the streets at night with vacuum cleaners strapped to their backs. I came across riotous pachinko parlors and heard tales of miniature octopus-on-a-stick snacks with hard-boiled eggs stuck into their heads. Bright plastic food was on display everywhere—even in the fancy restaurants.

Good fortune cats, *maneki-neko*, beckoned with raised paws from every single cash register in the country. In case you're wondering, a raised right paw attracts money and good fortune, while a raised left invites friendship and customers. Almost all the maneki-neko I saw had a raised right paw, which I guess was in line with ongoing retail priorities, although it might simply have reflected the then-current economy. I didn't see any with both paws raised, which I assume would attract money from one's friends, and would not be in keeping with common courtesy, let alone Japan's elevated arts of etiquette.

Those centuries-old lucky cats were the forbears of the *kawaii* or "cuteness" culture that originated in Japan and exploded in the 1990s, spreading around the world to produce billion-dollar sellers like Pokémon and Hello Kitty. It's a concept with a complicated history and many subgenres, including *erokawaii* (erotic cute), *fuwakawaii* (fluffy cute) and *yamikawaii* (dark and sickly cute).

Even if I didn't understand it, kawaii permeated everyday life: Gigantic ice cream cones with human feet waltzed in and out of storefronts; grown men wore manga neckties; banks, airlines and even police departments employed cartoon characters in their appeals to the public.

The Japanese fascination with automation added an unnerving aspect to my visit: Toto toilets greeted me with music and a console full of mysterious buttons offering more pulsation and temperature options for water, air and deodorant than any Westerner could possibly wrangle. Vending machines, popularized because of the high cost of labor and real estate in crowded Japanese cities, provided goods at the rate of one machine for every twenty-three people.

Beverages were big. Beer, sake, coffee and tea, juices and sodas— not to mention the very-popular-though-unappetizingly-named drink called Pocari Sweat—could be had anywhere for a few coins. Machines were also stocked with long-shelf-life staples like batteries and umbrellas, as well as less-expected products such as fresh apple slices, pet beetles and ladies' underwear, both new and used.

There's an unusual kinship with wildlife in Japan, too. Oddly alluring badgers marked the entrances to restaurants, and fox shrines dotted the landscape—reminders of the importance of nature spirits in the indigenous Shinto religion. On Miyajima

Island I mingled with the famous Sitka deer that roamed from visitor to visitor, sniffing our pockets for food and also nibbling on camera straps, paper bags and anything else that looked like it might be tasty. Another island, Okunoshima, was overrun with adorable feral rabbits—lie down on the ground and the furry creatures will pile up on top of you looking for treats. And they say the monkeys bathe in hot tubs up in Nagano Prefecture.

It wasn't until after I returned from my trip that Mom—of course it was Mom—sent me an odd book called *The Bento Box of Unuseless Japanese Inventions*. It explained a lot about Japanese culture. A fat full-color volume with a bright pink cover, it was written by Kenji Kawakami, who had invented a thing called *chindogu*.

Kawakami's idea arose back in the 1990s when he worked as an editor for a home-shopping magazine, *Mail Order Life*, aimed at Japanese suburban housewives. One month—as a joke—Kawakami used a few extra pages to showcase prototypes for outlandish products, for which he coined the term *chindogu*— literally "weird tool." Soon the Japanese public was hooked on the catalog, searching it eagerly for products like Wide Angle Eye Glasses ("Make tiny apartments into castles"), the Drymobile ("Your laundry dries as you drive your car") and Duster Slippers for Cats ("Now the most boring job around the house becomes hours of fun … for your cat!").

One of my favorite chindogu is featured on the cover of the book. It's called the Hay Fever Hat. A toilet paper dispenser loaded up with a fat roll of TP is affixed to the top of a user's head by means of a plastic headdress secured with an elastic chin strap. The paper extends over the forehead and is ready, by virtue of such proximity, for instant use. When pulled down a mere few inches, the paper squares are perfectly positioned in front of and slightly below the nose. If the toilet paper is draped correctly, the wearer can still see with both eyes. When the need for paper is over, the roll remains handy atop the wearer's head, ready for the next sniffle or sneeze.

The chindogu concept quickly became so popular it threatened to get out of hand, so Kawakami and his collaborators formed the International Chindogu Society and developed the Ten Tenets of Chindogu in order to clarify for enthusiastic adherents just what did—and what did not—qualify.

I learned all about this in the *Unuseless Inventions* book. Tenet Number One: A chindogu must be (almost) completely useless. If you invent something that turns out to be so handy you use it all the time, then you have failed to make a chindogu. That was reinforced by Tenet Number Five: Chindogu are not for sale. They may not even be sold as a joke, as it turns out. If money changes hands, you have violated the spirit of chindogu and thereby disqualified your invention.

This ethos is further amplified by Tenet Number Three: Inherent in every chindogu is the spirit of anarchy. Chindogu are man-made objects that have broken free from the chains of usefulness. They exist for their own sake, rather than depending on cultural or practical utility. Additional characteristics of true chindogu are that they must actually exist but may not be patented or sold; must be a tool for everyday life rather than for specialized use; and must never favor one race or religion over another.

Headgear holds a prominent place in the chindogu pantheon. The Zip-Up Cold Mask—a surgical face mask with a horizontal zipper across the middle—offers easy oral access for a straw or a cigarette. I could envision using one of these myself, but the addition of a zipper would negate its N95 rating. And although it does provide a handy way to drink while keeping germs at bay, the claim that it's also useful for dining takes things a bit too far. Perhaps that is the very attribute that qualifies this accessory as "un-useless."

One of the most popular chindogu are the Umbrella Shoe Savers, miniature umbrellas that fasten to the toe of each shoe, providing excellent protection from precipitation, although the width of the umbrellas means the wearer must take care not to bring her feet too close together when walking, lest she risk tripping and possibly ruining her shoes in that manner.

Many chindogu are designed for people who are napping on their way to work, which is a "thing" in Japan. Apparently, it is the mark of a proudly dedicated and profoundly overworked salaryman and is okay, or even admirable, as long as one is well dressed and of a certain age. (It is important to be positioned as if one has simply drifted off to sleep sitting up, because comfort, slouching and blankets are never appropriate in public.) Enter the Subway Sleeper's Chin Stand, a handy helper for citizens who are catching a few Zs on the train. It consists of a small-but-sturdy tripod fitted at the top with a cushioned, U-shaped chin-holder—something like a miniature pool noodle—that promises to support the wearer's entire body, allowing her to nap in comfort during the rush hour crunch. It is easily adjusted for either sitting or standing users of any height or weight "and can also be taken to boring cocktail parties."

Kawakami loved these off-kilter creations partly because they mocked the slick and efficient IT culture that exploded in Japan in the 1990s. You want progress? How about an electric fork that automatically twirls your spaghetti—even if it splatters a little tomato sauce onto your face? When seen in that way, as a response to the country's relentless focus on productivity, chindogu and kawaii seem like inevitable developments in Japanese culture.

While an appreciation of kawaii eludes me, I adore the concept of chindogu and felt sad that they don't exist in the real world—until I got to page 250 of the un-useless inventions book. There I came upon the Self-Portrait Camera Stick, a twenty-two-inch, telescoping, camera-holding pole …

Wait a minute—that's a selfie stick!

Yes, it's true: The selfie stick gets a two-page spread in *The Bento Box of Unuseless Japanese Inventions*. For those who appreciate historical context, the book was first published in 2005. In fact, the selfie stick also appeared a decade earlier in an identical two-page spread in the 1995 book called *101 Unuseless Japanese Inventions: The Art of Chindogu*, also by Kenji Kawakami. The telescoping self-portrait pole was patented in 2005 and became commercially available in the United States in 2006. However, it remained truly un-useless (the pole "could become a tiresome feature of your photo album") for less than a year. Apple brought out the iPhone in 2007, and suddenly it was everywhere. Who could have guessed such a universally un-useless item would be picked up by the masses and go on to become one of *Time* magazine's Twenty-Five Best Inventions of 2014? Who could have guessed that less than one year later, in November 2015, Silicon Valley tech leaders would name the selfie stick and nuclear weapons as the two technologies they would most like to un-invent?

Mom died in 2011, too soon to see the selfie stick attain that universally useful status, but she would have loved the ridiculousness of a camera on a stick becoming so commonplace it had to be de-listed as chindogu.

Mom—free spirit and cultural explorer—that one's for you!

"Crow on a Branch" woodblock print by Kawanabe Kyosai

Autumn on Spirit Mountain

MJ Pramik

late autumn quiet
crows rule the morning
　　side streets empty

the long night is through
dawn lights the paths for walking
　　crows watch and wait

winter approaches
the city awaits the first snow
　　meteor showers

hummingbirds call out
waiting for the mist to lift
    we too wait for this

there on the city street
autumn air grabs my face
    mountain haze of fog

a dog barks far off
only once then, air humming,
    we sit waiting

harvest moon hidden
by fog and trees and buildings
    no frogs, no water

still alive, I am
walking through the autumn day
    searching marigolds

looking for a friend
this lonely autumn evening
    the fog hides the moon

smell of old drawer
awakens the morning light
    invisible life

walk among cedars
around the blackened spire
    would my spine stand so

early to mailbox
the day's adventure begun
    jackhammer serene

Courses in a kaiseki meal

BOWING TO WASHOKU
Anne Sigmon

This was it—the last chance to prove to myself that I was foodie enough to appreciate the healthy deliciousness of one of the world's great cuisines.

I almost missed it. Tucked into my twenty-eighth-floor room in Tokyo's Conrad Hotel after a long day at the end of a hectic week, I was just about to order room service pasta when the phone rang. It was Tania, my friend and traveling companion. This was the last night before we headed home.

"Do you have plans for dinner?" she asked. "There's a sushi bar in the hotel. I hear it's pretty good."

Ah, sushi. There it was: one last chance. I'd tried everything else. "I'd love to go."

Three months earlier, when I'd signed on with friends for a whirlwind tour of Japan, I was drawn to the ancient art and culture —tenth-century calligraphy, painted screens, delicate silk kimonos. I wanted to see them all.

What I didn't crave was the food. It wasn't the awkward chopsticks, the stir-fry or even the raw fish that's always put me off

Japanese cuisine. It's that bonito-fishy-seaweedy taste—a bitter, greenish flavor that reminds me of slogging in a leaky rowboat through a dirty tide.

Rather than starve, I stocked up in advance on protein bars. The night before I left, I struggled to cram bars into the corners of my already-bulging suitcase. Maybe I could stuff a few into my shoes? Then I stopped myself. Instead of avoiding Japanese food, why not teach myself to like it?

I'd read that Japanese cuisine (called *washoku*) is so beloved that UNESCO accorded it World Heritage status, one of only four national cuisines so honored. I was embarrassed to be the only one in my circle of friends who didn't love Japanese food. Surely familiarity would ignite a flame. With only that vague idea, I set off to Tokyo, the world's most Michelin-starred city and one of the most artful food scenes on the planet.

Day One did not begin well. Slimy greens, congealed noodle soup, a dark liquid swimming with tiny tentacles and dead eyes staring—the Asian breakfast buffet at my Tokyo hotel was not the best introduction to Japanese dining. Despite my vow to embrace Japanese food, the sight of those fish eyes on the buffet sent me scurrying to the omelet bar on the other side of the restaurant. There, I fortified myself with eggs, bacon and a mound of fresh fruit topped off with hot coffee and a buttery croissant. *I'll get to the Japanese food later,* I promised myself.

But first there'd be a group tour of the Tsukiji Fish Market, scheduled for 8 a.m., our trip leader, Marian, told us. I dreaded the idea of a morning visit—a good time to see the market in action, yes, but, I knew from experience, too early for me to appreciate the sight and smell of all that piscine carnage.

28

Stupefying in scale, Tsukiji (pronounced *skee-gee*) Market was an eighty-year-old jumble of concrete and metal buildings, bays and loading docks in various states of dilapidation. Sprawling over fifty-seven acres, it's the largest wholesale fish market in the world,* moving five million pounds of seafood every day.

Inside the vast market, the floor was wet with melted ice, fish slime and blood dripping from wooden chopping tables. Men in rubber boots and long, plastic aprons shouted orders. Narrow aisles teemed with scooters, handcarts and buyers toting woven bamboo baskets. Motorized turret trucks hauling pallets of fish bore down on us from every direction. Our guide's thin voice was lost in the bedlam. The place was jammed with fifty-gallon blue and white plastic coolers, wooden barrels and metal ice tables packed with sea creatures: bluefin tuna (*ahi*—the undisputed king) as well as eel (*unagi*), mackerel (*saba*), smelt (*shishamo*), and four hundred other species of fish (so the guide told us) that I couldn't begin to identify. As our one-hour tour stretched into overtime, I tried to ignore the stink and the gore; the white, slimy squid with tiny, reproachful black eyes; and the google-eyed sea bream that seemed to look up at me in horror. I focused instead on the prettier offerings—pink octopus arms that reminded me of pop art, black spiny sea urchins, crabs, clams, live oysters and big conchs in trumpet-shaped shells.

Outside, specialty shops sold everything from handmade knives to bamboo strainers to dried kelp (*kombu*) and thin flakes of fermented and smoked bonito fish (*katsuobushi*). Those last two, I learned, are the "magic ingredients" of Japanese cuisine, lending their flavor to dashi, the stock made from fish and kelp that's a staple of Japanese cooking.

*The fish market at Tsukiji was closed in 2018 and re-opened as Toyosu Market at a new location.

That savory flavor—recognized worldwide now as the fifth taste after sweet, sour, bitter and salty—was isolated in 1908 by a Tokyo professor experimenting with dashi. He called the new flavor *umami*—"deliciousness."

I shook my head in disappointment. I'd discovered the secret to magnificent Japanese food. Sadly, the "magic" was the same seaweedy-fishy taste that turned my stomach. Perhaps I'd need those power bars after all.

Normally not much of a shopper, I was happy to leave the fish market behind when our guide led our group to a row of boutiques in the nearby Ginza area. We window-shopped our way through a line of upmarket establishments to Nihonbashi Takashimaya, Japan's oldest department store. We'd have lunch at the food court there, she told us.

I was puzzled that she'd chosen a department store food court for lunch. I didn't know that these courts, called *depachika* ("department store basement"), are trendy purveyors of Japanese cuisine, selling everything from bento boxes to $100 white strawberries called *hatsukoi no kaori* ("scent of first love"). Depachika are so popular that many offer guided tours or concierges. But at the Takashimaya store, we were on our own. Our guide told us to fan out, grab something to eat, and meet at the cramped, table-and-stool setup where she'd managed to stake out a few places. I fell behind my companions, lost in the cavernous basement where I faced row upon row of glass counters that looked like jewelry displays at a New York diamond wholesaler. Each counter held a bewilderment of mysterious foodstuffs packed in tidy plastic containers along with flimsy wooden chopsticks. I didn't see bento boxes, sushi rolls or anything that looked familiar—

maybe I was in the wrong section? It's the way my husband might feel if I sent him to Nordstrom for an eye pencil. The signs in neat Japanese characters were no help. The only things I could read were the prices. High.

Running short on time, I gave up trying to make sense of it all. I sidled up to one of the counters, smiled at the attendant and pointed to the least slimy-fishy-looking morsel I could find—some sort of tiny pie that reminded me (vaguely) of a Cornish pasty.

After paying, I rejoined my friends, unwrapped my tidbit, gingerly grabbed an edge with my chopsticks and popped it into my mouth. Then I tried not to gag. The spongy, seaweedy substance was spicy-hot—something I'd hadn't expected; my mouth felt on fire, my throat constricted, and my stomach, ever sensitive to hot spice, heaved. That one bite was all I could manage.

So far my Japanese culinary experiment was a flop. Could I be that much of a rube? That hard to please? Most of the others in the group seemed to love the food. Why couldn't I?

By dinnertime I was ravenous.

"That's good," my friend Tania said. "This is the special kaiseki dinner. You'll love it."

Our destination for kaiseki was the Michelin-starred restaurant, Kozue, on the 40th floor of Tokyo's Park Hyatt Hotel. On the way up the elevator, we chatted about the hotel's movie moment as the location for Sofia Coppola's 2003 film *Lost in Translation*.

I forgot about food when I stepped off the elevator into the dark, amber elegance of the wood-paneled dining room—a serene, ultra-modern design paired with a view of towering Mount Fuji. This was about as far from the fish market as I could get.

I'd heard kaiseki described as a traditional multi-course meal.

"It's much more than that. It's the haute cuisine of Japan," our guide told us as we followed a petite hostess in an opulent silk kimono to a long table by the window. "Its roots go deep into the past, to the traditions of the Imperial Court, to samurai cultures as well as the Buddhist monastery and the tea ceremony."

Once our group settled at the table, our waitress bowed as she served sake and distributed a copy of the set menu they had selected for us. It was long—nine courses. Our waitress explained that kaiseki dining is about fresh local ingredients of the season. "It's the chef's job," she said, "to appeal to all the senses." A kaiseki menu also showcases the different cooking methods, from raw sashimi and sushi to grilled, boiled and steamed. Even the dinnerware is important. At Kozue, cups and porcelain are selected from Chef Oe's private collection: bold black and red pottery plates, chunky green bowls that look like lotus leaves, delicate china bowls of ice to display the sashimi.

The room enchanted me: the dim lighting, the quiet elegance. I wanted to relax into the warmth of the sake and the graceful care of our waitress. But how would I manage the food? Each course looked like a still life from a Japanese art book: slices of fish paired with a tiny kumquat and graceful green buttons of wasabi … a sushi platter decorated with cucumber and a round of dragonfruit … a cooking pot that resembled a volcano. Each was embellished with tiny leaves, twigs or edible flowers. I hesitated to desecrate these masterpieces with my clumsy chopstick technique. However, in deference to hunger, I persisted.

Some of these morsels were nirvana: succulent ahi, kobe beef with a tangy sauce, small, dewy shrimp. But in between, the tiny tree-shaped stands of nori (seaweed), the boiled course of dashi-based soup, the miniscule tentacle-shaped sea creature with beady eyes, broke the spell.

I was a washoku castoff. I'd had the best of traditional Japanese cooking, been treated to the ultimate deliciousness, and still failed to love.

It was no surprise that the next stop on our tour presented even greater gastronomic challenges.

It took three trains and a cable car to reach our destination 2,600 feet up on the side of a craggy, cedar-forested slope southwest of Osaka. It was the sacred Mount Koya, Koyasan, a 1,200-year-old complex of more than a hundred temples and monasteries, the center of the Shingon school of Esoteric Buddhism. As one of the most sacred sites in Japan, Koyasan has attracted pilgrims for centuries.

We'd come to stay at Henjoson-in, one of the fifty-two Buddhist temples that offer *shukubo* (pilgrims' lodgings). Here, we'd retreat into the world of the spirits, stroll in mystical gardens, visit ancient shrines and attend meditation and prayers. We'd also sleep on tatami mats and eat *shogin ryori*, the restrained Buddhist devotional cuisine that is one of most celebrated of Japanese cooking styles.

I'd read what to expect from a shojin ryori meal: soup, rice, a few vegetable sides and pickles. The main ingredients would be tofu and local vegetables seasoned with dashi and miso—twin nemeses in my quest to become a gastronome of Japanese cooking.

Breakfast in the austere dining room tested my resolve. I missed my morning coffee, and sitting on the floor was a trial to my back. The cheery blue and white dishes lifted my spirits until I sniffed the telltale miso-seaweedy, tofu-y concoctions. I went for the boiled

33

egg, the rice with a bit of soy and some marinated carrots. To avoid humiliation, I nudged the other items around in their dainty little dishes, hoping no one would notice how little I ate.

On the trip back to Tokyo, our group split up. Some stopped in Kyoto, others in Osaka or Hiroshima. I went straight back to Tokyo to check into the hotel for our last night, feeling dejected that the trip was ending and I'd failed in my quest to bond with Japanese food. Then Tania called with the invitation to sushi.

Stepping into Kazahana Restaurant was like floating on air: Zen-inspired, minimalist design, a light sea-green color palette, and floor-to-ceiling windows twenty-eight stories above the garden below. The hostess, looking like a geisha in a silk kimono, wide obi and *sakkō* hairstyle, bowed as we entered. She showed us to a bright-white, eight-chair sushi bar sectioned off from the restaurant proper by a translucent wall. Tania and I had the bar to ourselves, tended by two exuberant young chefs in white coats and soda-jerk hats. There were no menus. They didn't speak much English. We spoke no Japanese.

"Just surprise us," Tania said, committing our evening to the fates.

Without knowing it, we'd just invoked *omakase* (literally "I will leave it to you"), a Japanese tradition of asking that the chef select your order.

"Sake?" the older chef asked.

"Oh, yes!"

There followed an hours-long blur of flashing knives and slices of fish so fresh that I half expected them to wiggle in my hands: some silky, some firm-textured, some with rice, some without. The chefs seasoned them to sublimity with soy, soba, grated ginger, wasabi or simply salt and pepper. There was a delicate ramekin of *chirashi*, rice topped with slices of bluefin tuna and vegetables. There was *nigiri-sushi*—hand-pressed rice topped by a slice of fish—and sashimi, pieces of fish topped with roe and spring onions. Using instruments so delicate they looked like they belonged in a surgical suite, our heroes embellished the morsels of fish with tidbits of bright-colored vegetables—dainty slices of carrot, sprigs of onion—and arranged them on carefully-selected plates. I was euphoric—I'd never tasted anything so good. At some point in the evening a lobster was involved. Later we devoured a light, crisp tempura.

Although (I learned later) a full sushi omakase menu generally involves at least one broth course, I don't remember one that night. Perhaps the chef decided to spare us. Or maybe, by then, I'd learned to ignore the broth. Freed from the bitter seaweed taste I'd found impossible to like, I explored the full deliciousness of the ultra-fresh fish, the tangy sauces and contrasting flavors of the vegetable garnishes.

Tania and I were so captivated with our dinner we bought the chefs a round of sake. They returned the favor. Back and forth we toasted, sharing no language other than laughter, the universal dialect of shared appreciation and fun. Tania and I were the last customers to leave the restaurant that night.

Finally, in that sushi bar full of bonhomie and gratitude, with no dashi in sight, I'd discovered my personal washoku—a Japanese cuisine I could love.

Fish on ice at Tsukiji Market

GHOSTS OF TSUKIJI

Lenny Karpman

Tsukiji Fish Market was, for many years, the world's largest wholesaler of fish and seafood, selling five million pounds of briny wonderfulness every day. From 1935 to 2018, when it was permanently closed, Tsukiji was a vital center of life in Tokyo. The residents miss it—and so do I, because I once worked there. On a recent trip to Tokyo I ventured out to visit the market, for what I didn't realize would be the last time.

Jet lag had sent me to bed early. I awakened at 4:30 in the morning, about the time my tour companions staggered in from the bar. As they fell into bed, I tiptoed out, heading into the night with "Tsukiji Market" written in Japanese on the back of a card and the name and address of my hotel on the front. Confident that the little Japanese I had learned would carry me through, I greeted the cabby with a polite honorific salutation; he grunted and rasped a totally unintelligible guttural response. I asked where we were, and he grunted, "Niu Otani Hoteru"—the name of the hotel. I asked the direction we were heading, and he grunted again, "Tsukiji Sakana-ya," the name of the fish market. No more conversation, no more information.

There was little traffic on the black streets of Tokyo at that hour, until the taxi neared the Tsukiji Fish Market. As we approached the market, we passed battalions of small trucks and divisions of motorized carts. My driver grunted one last time and deposited me in front of a maze of buildings that looked like airport hangers. There were fires in metal trashcans, marking the route and warming hands. I joined the processional and marched in. I was out of uniform, without pant legs tucked into knee-high rubber boots and with a camera hung from the neck of my bright pumpkin-colored flannel shirt.

The shadowy figures became illuminated as they entered the vast halls, but the colors of the fishmonger army hardly changed in the soft light. They wore only shades of gray, dark blue or black—jackets, pants, sweatshirts and sweaters. They sloshed in black boots. The tons of block ice made it colder inside than out. Narrow, wet aisles separated small stalls, each selling one or two items. Wooden boxes and stainless-steel trays full of glistening, slippery harvest from the sea sat edge-to-edge on tables illuminated by blue-white neon that made it all even more surreal. Some had razor-sharp predator's teeth and some wore faces befitting a Star Wars bar scene. Three kinds of eel squirmed in glistening tangles, and more colors and sizes of shrimp than I had ever imagined created a fantastic mandala. Sea cucumbers, cockles, jellyfish, yellow and green grouper, red snapper, yellowtail and barracuda, small squid and huge squid all stretched out before me, flanked by cuttlefish and octopus, raw and cooked. Those that were cooked were white-fleshed inside and dark red outside if they had been pickled, or golden if they had been cooked in soy. The variety of fish roe, too, was incredible: silver gray, pale yellow, iridescent orange, golden and crimson. These delicacies were displayed mounded and unadorned, clinging like barnacles to strips of seaweed or encased like sausages in semi-transparent tubes. Seaweed came in all shades of green, from lime to dark forest, and in black, brown and dark purple. The clams, oysters, scallops and crabs went from teaspoon-tiny to platter-large. There were miniature periwinkles and giant conchs.

The vendors were generally friendly and much more communicative than the cabby had been. A few did produce a deep-throated growl on occasion, as if to accentuate a word or phrase. They seemed amused by my exuberance and curiosity and answered my questions as slowly and as simply as if they were responding to an inquisitive toddler.

Closer to dockside stood dozens of large tables with electric bandsaws. Workers in surgical gloves and rubber aprons operated on 200-pound headless and tailless frozen tuna bodies. They cut the tuna lengthwise along their backbones, then loaded them onto carts for delivery to the buyers' mini-trucks waiting outside. The place sounded like a sawmill.

One vendor, who had been patient with me and had struggled to welcome me in English two hours before, smiled at me and bowed slightly as I tried to find my way out. He had exhausted his English with his greeting, but was adept at charades. I returned his smile and his bow, carefully bending my head a little more than he had, as a sign of respect. "*Sumimasen*"—Excuse me. "New Otani Hotel, *doko desu ka*"—where is it? "*Yukuri, kudasai*"—Slowly, please. I handed him the card with the hotel's name, and we both tried our best. The hotel was not nearby, however. He tried to draw me a little map but seemed unwilling to give it to me because it was rough and not to scale. He was a stern self-critic and kept apologizing. He frowned and tucked his chin under the neck of his black windbreaker. I apologized for disturbing him and thanked him as profusely as my limited language skills allowed. I was going to take my leave when we both said, "*Gomen nasai*"—I am sorry—in unison, as if we had been rehearsing. Both of our faces erupted into ear-to-ear smiles. I extended my hand. He took it in his and accepted the bond of a handshake. And then my new friend became resolute; he raised his chin high, puffed out his chest and chuckled deep in his throat. He obviously had hatched a plan. He asked me if I knew Japanese numbers. I nodded *yes*. He asked me to count, and I counted to twenty, then by tens to 100. He smiled and bowed slightly. He then opened his cash box, gave me a large bill and directed me to change places with him. He pointed to the golden, soy-cooked octopus pieces in the metal tray and slowly articulated an order: "*Tako, ichi kiro han, kudasai.*" I got the message. I lifted a plastic bag onto the scale, pretended to fill it and pressed my index finger down to move the needle on the dial to 1.5 kilograms. I calculated the cost, took the bill, gave him change and presented him the empty bag with a bow and a "Thank you very much." Mr. Yamamoto introduced himself and so did I, repeating each other's names aloud and exchanging salutations. He then rather abruptly hurried away and left me behind the counter to tend his money and tentacled wares. I surmised that he had gone off to find an English speaker to give me directions.

A small gray-haired woman in a long dark raincoat walked by three times. The first time she stole a glance out of the corner of her eye as she stepped by in her plastic rain shoes. The second time she paused ever so slightly, then, after a closer look, quickened her pace and turned away.

Finally, she stopped and whispered in a high falsetto that she wanted half a kilo of the octopus. Her eyes darted back and forth from the octopus to her purse to the scale, but she avoided my eyes. She extracted exact change and handed it to me from the greatest distance possible. She watched the scale as I put successive pieces into the plastic bag with metal pincers. When I reached the half-kilo mark, she inhaled barely audibly and bowed her head almost imperceptibly. I handed her the package with a bow, a thank-you and a smile. Her eyes were trapped and she smiled back. She placed her package into a crocheted shopping bag. She seemed very pleased with herself for her courageous purchase from the bearded gaijin in the loud shirt. Me too! I noted the sale on a small pad next to the plastic bags. I would have affixed a gold star had there been one.

Mr. Yamamoto returned with a little boy who was barely visible in a down jacket and a knitted ski cap and gloves. The lad could have been six or seven. He hopped up on the wooden stool and took my place. Before I could figure out how to brag about my sale without destroying my veneer of humility, Yamamoto-san was steering me down the aisle. We walked briskly through two cavernous buildings and out a door into an alley.

We negotiated the maze to and over the bridge and onto a commercial street with open-fronted shops selling shaved bonito flakes, sushi, noodles, pottery and kitchen utensils. He walked quickly and silently. I had to press to keep abreast. At each turn he smiled at me and angled his head a few degrees in our new direction. We descended into the subway. He bought two tickets from a vending machine and we were off.

My guide seemed less willing to play charades with me in this public place than he had in the partial privacy of his fish stand. He used hand signals to beckon me in and out of the spanking-clean subway cars. With his hand open, palm facing downward, he flexed his four fingers toward his palm two or three times rapidly, signaling me to follow. I tracked very closely behind him and marveled at his agile figure, walking rapidly but never touching another human, even with the brush of a sleeve or elbow. We exited onto a busy street in an upscale neighborhood. I resumed my position at his side, a quarter of a pace behind, like an obedient dog who had been instructed to heel. A boy on a bicycle with a four-foot-tall bundle of magazines on the back beat us through the crosswalk. A few blocks later, we arrived at the door of the hotel.

Yamamoto-san refused payment for even the subway tickets. I offered him a drink inside, but he politely declined. We repeated our bows and handshakes. He gave me his business card, which I could not read, and I gave him my business card, which he could not read. "*Sayonara, dewa mata*"—Goodbye, until next time, he said. Then he hurried away down the drive toward the street, without a backward glance. Inside the lobby, the clock read 10:45. My tourmates were heading into a breakfast buffet.

"Where did you go?"

"To the fish market."

"Why would anyone want to go to a fish market? Didn't it stink?"

I donned the requisite smile and nodded my head, not to affirm, but to leave them, politely. "Sayonara," I said softly, but from a deeper, raspier part of my throat. That is how we, the working men of Tokyo, speak.

Wagyu, handled with care

THE WAY OF WAGYU

Laurie McAndish King

I've sampled unusual foods all around the world: blood pudding, haggis, kangaroo, crocodile, even horsemeat. And while I am not generally a meat eater, though that list of sampled foods suggests otherwise, I had heard that Kobe beef is the most delicious beef in the world—tender and buttery, with an exquisite texture. So, when I learned that I'd be traveling to Japan for a business trip I set a modest goal for the little free time I would enjoy. I wanted to taste Kobe beef.

So did my husband, Jim, who accompanied me. And, because my personal plans sometimes go awry on tightly scheduled visits, we slipped it in right at the beginning of our itinerary: To motivate ourselves to stay up, adjust to local time and vanquish jet lag, we'd made reservations for a special Kobe beef dinner to look forward to on our first evening in Kyoto.

Unfortunately, I was already hungry when we landed at Osaka Kansai International Airport. It was four o'clock in the afternoon, and after our twelve-hour flight I was fighting off low-blood-sugar malaise. I needed to find food, fast.

And there it was, before we were even out of the airport: a Japanese fast-food court. The long row of storefronts looked pretty much the same as they do at home: gleaming stainless steel, fluorescent lights, and lots of red and yellow posters with large photos of appetizing yet unnaturally colorful foods. The restaurants were staffed by earnest young people dressed in bright yellow shirts, red-and-white checked aprons, and red hats with snappy white piping. That universally familiar, unfailingly tempting fried-food aroma wafted through the air.

On one side of the aisle an establishment called "Taco Tacos" looked promising, but I didn't really trust anyone in Japan to do a good job with Mexican food. Across the way, smiling servers from various stalls made crepes, cooked rows of decoratively slashed hot dogs in a shallow pool of fat, and roasted long ears of corn. I paused, however, in front of a hamburger stand.

"Don't eat here—it's a greasy spoon!" Jim warned wisely. "And remember, tonight is our Kobe beef night. You'll regret it if you eat now."

"No, I won't; I'm starving and it's hours before dinnertime. This looks fine to me," I snapped in low-blood-sugar defiance.

I got a hamburger—single patty, no cheese, one limp piece of iceberg—and downed it quickly, just to take the edge off. The meat was dry and flavorless, with the mouthfeel of limp-but-chewy cardboard and a long, complex aftertaste that effortlessly married grease and MSG. I felt temporarily satisfied, but sure enough a few minutes later as we boarded a bus to the hotel, a tinge of nausea began to roil my belly. To distract myself I reviewed what my pre-trip research about Kobe beef had turned up.

First of all, it was amazing to discover that Kobe Bryant was named after Kobe beef! I'm still wondering why anyone would name their little baby after a beef product, even if it is tender and succulent and the world's most *revered* beef product. But that's all I know about that story.

I also learned about both Kobe and Wagyu beef. The terms are often used interchangeably, but that is not quite correct usage. Wagyu is a reference to any of four breeds of Japanese cattle: "Wa" means Japanese or Japanese-style, and "gyu" refers to cattle. Just as fine wine is marked—and marketed—with its appellation, Wagyu is generally sold using the name of the area it comes from, such as Matsusaka or Omi or Kobe, and Kobe beef is indisputably the best, for reasons I will soon explain.

It is a rare dish. To begin with, beef itself is not all that common in Japan. A nation of islands, the country has always depended on seafood for protein. Pastureland was in short supply, and because they needed draft animals—cattle—to cultivate the rice that made up such a large part of the Japanese diet, eating beef didn't make economic sense. In fact, it was downright wasteful.

In the year 675, Emperor Tenmu outlawed eating the meat of cattle, horse, dog, chicken or monkey. This dictate was a practical matter, but it was also in alignment with Shinto as well as with Buddhism, which had recently been introduced to Japan and discouraged meat-eating because of ... well, if you were committed to showing compassion to all living beings, not to mention if you believed in reincarnation, you might not eat meat, either. You might even come to think meat-eaters were barbarians, as the Japanese did for many centuries.

Shinto priests deemed a person unclean for 150 days after they ate meat; their penance was a 100-day fast. Further, any person who ate *with* someone who had eaten meat had to fast for twenty-one days, and anyone who ate with a person who ate with someone else who had consumed meat was ordered to fast for seven days. Wild animals and birds may have been exceptions—and there are always exceptions for the well-to-do—but eating beef or horsemeat during that time was unthinkable.

That was pretty much the situation for some twelve hundred years until January of 1872, when Emperor Meiji dared to eat meat in public. Local monks believed this constituted an existential crisis that would destroy the soul of the Japanese people, and chaos ensued, but the door had been opened.

The real turning point came when the United States occupied Japan after WWII, from 1945 to 1952, during which time the Supreme Commander of the Allied Powers, charged with caring for a starving populace, implemented a school lunch program that introduced animal protein to eight million children. (It also provided a tremendous boost to the US meat industry.)

Some of these children began to see this formerly taboo choice—and many things American, for that matter—as a way to push boundaries and as a cool rebellion against traditional culture. Even Japanese beef-themed apparel became a stylish, youth-driven trend, influenced, no doubt, by Lady Gaga's beef-as-a-statement meat outfit (dress, hat, purse and boots made of actual raw flank steak), which she wore at the 2010 MTV Video Music Awards. I've recently found online offerings of "Wagyu Beef Meat Print Leather Boots," for example, and the "Wagyu Beef Meat Print Bodysuit, women's, long-sleeved," alongside hoodies, bomber jackets, underwear and automotive seat covers. These are actual products whose surfaces are suffused with photographic likenesses of raw beef.

In the case of Wagyu products, however, the centuries-old tradition of kaiseki also came into play. In this form of dining, beautiful and elaborately prepared multi-course meals are a tangible representation—if only briefly—of the great care that is taken with all ingredients in Japanese cuisine. That extends, in the case of Kobe beef, to the entire lives of the cattle involved.

What ends up being certified as this esteemed culinary specialty must begin as pure-bred stock from the ancient, black-haired Tajima strain of Wagyu cattle. It must also—and why does this not surprise me?—be a virgin. These cattle will not be slaughtered; they will be sacrificed.

Each cow is numbered and tracked individually throughout its life. In addition to belonging to this venerated lineage and leading a certified-sex-free life, the basic rules are that the individual must be born and raised exclusively in the Kobe region of Hyōgo Prefecture, fed only on grains and grasses that were also grown within the prefecture, and upon its death, it must be processed in one of the approved slaughterhouses located in the prefecture. It must end up with a maximum gross carcass weight of 470 kilograms—just over 1,000 pounds. High "meat quality scores" and "marbling ratios" are also required.

That may all sound a bit precious, but it's only the beginning. There are intriguing rumors about exactly how the cattle are fed and raised, but the actual process is a mystery to many. Kobe livestock are raised on fewer than 300 small farms, the largest of which generally pasture only ten to fifteen animals, so each individual gets plenty of attention. The livestock are apparently fed beer from a bottle during the sweltering summer months to keep their appetites up. And during their final days, the cattle may ingest hefty quantities of beer mash. Of course they are fat—very fat! But are they really massaged with sake every day in order to make their meat more tender? Would a taste test reveal any difference between a kneaded rump and one that had been ignored?

I grew up in rural Iowa, where many of my friends lived on family farms, some with herds of cattle. Every year the 4H kids raised calves—lovingly and respectfully, for the most part—so beef was not an uncommon topic of conversation. People had surprisingly strong opinions about it, but arguments mainly revolved around how much blood was too much blood on the plate. There was absolutely no question, though, that marbled, corn-fed beef was the best you could eat. In the kitchen, before it was broiled, the long, white ribbons of fat looked almost festive as they rippled through Christmas-red flesh on a good T-bone steak.

The fat in Kobe beef is completely different than that. First of all, it is scattershot—tiny globules are evenly dispersed throughout the meat, as though it had been sprayed with a miniature BB gun. And we're talking *lots* of fat—Kobe beef's ratio of marbled fat to meat can be ten times higher than it is for other breeds. Because of that high fat content and its distinctive marbling, it's sometimes referred to as "white steak."

Kobe fat has particularly high levels of monounsaturated omega fatty acids—the healthy kind that tend to increase a person's levels of HDL, or "good" cholesterol, and lower their LDLs. Compared with saturated fat, it has been correlated with lower inflammation levels and improved insulin sensitivity in humans. So, one *could* make the argument that Kobe beef is a health food, if one were so inclined.

But in the end, it's all about chemistry. That is the real secret of Kobe beef, the reason it exhibits an entirely different type of tenderness than the textural quality we expect from, say, a tenderloin filet. The specific type of fat in Kobe beef melts at a low temperature—including when it's inside your mouth, sitting on your tongue. The ideal way to cook this delicacy, therefore, is in a very hot pan that will char the outside of the cut while leaving the center ready to literally melt in your mouth, like butter.

And that is exactly what I got that evening at the Kobe beef restaurant in the Taruya district of downtown Kyoto. I don't recall its name, but the interior was unforgettable: tiny private rooms, gorgeous arrangements of fresh flowers, indirect up-lighting. The distant murmurs of other diners were just loud enough to reassure us that we weren't the only patrons that evening. The service was superb. This was a huge splurge. I ordered the least expensive Kobe option on the menu, and calculated it would cost US$48 per bite.

"Forty-eight dollars a bite!" Jim gulped. "Are you sure …?"

"It's a once-in-a-lifetime experience," I insisted.

"Is it served by royal butlers, on a solid gold plate? One we can take home and melt down to pay for the dinner?"

When it arrived, the Kobe beef was served on a small, hand-thrown plate, just three little morsels. They didn't look remotely like a good Iowa steak would. This meat was very pale, and we would never *pre-cut* it into pieces like that, unless we were serving it to children who had not yet developed their knife skills.

"Hmmm. They look quite succulent," Jim observed. "And the outside is nicely charred."

I picked up the first plump, bite-sized piece with my chopsticks and examined it, looking for an outward sign of its inner glory.

"How are we supposed to know if the inside is cooked?" Jim continued. "Are you going to cut through a piece to see?"

He was teasing me. The pieces were so small they could hardly be said to *have* an inside. Even if they had one, I would never see it because these were intended to be popped into one's mouth whole, like sushi. And I couldn't imagine trying to cut a piece of steak—even an exceptionally tender and succulent one like this—using only a pair of chopsticks.

With what I believed was appropriate gravitas for the moment, I ceremoniously moved the first Kobe morsel to a spot beneath my nose and inhaled. The aroma was definitely umami: steak-y with a whiff of soy sauce. I popped the bite into my mouth and chewed slowly. The mild flavor and high fat content were immediately apparent, and the meat really did seem to melt on my tongue; it was the strangest feeling. I closed my eyes and after two or three chews the beef disappeared.

I was just beginning to feel indignant that I'd only had a short moment to enjoy that fleeting succulence when suddenly the unique fat from the Kobe joined the lingering grease from the burger, and my digestive system became, shall we say, *overloaded*. The problem arose after two bites (US$96!) and I did my best not to disrupt the refined ambience of the place as I leapt up from my chair and trotted furtively to the restroom, which was gorgeous— dark purple walls, single white orchid—where I upchucked.

Fortunately, I was the only person in the small room, so I was able to berate myself in privacy: *How could you have done such a stupid thing? Your one chance, probably in a lifetime, to eat Kobe beef, and you've failed because of your bad decision, a choice driven by something as mundane and transitory as minor hunger pangs. Worse than failing—you've succeeded, but then upended your success, ruined the evening for Jim and wasted US$96. And what about the cow? The noble bovine gave up sex and ultimately sacrificed its very life so you could taste a bite of its flesh—yet you enjoyed it for only a few seconds. It didn't strengthen your body or elevate your soul ....*

But then I talked myself down: *Oh, snap out of it, girl! You can make it through the rest of dinner. Just don't look at any food and you'll be fine.*

I rinsed my face. My nausea had completely disappeared, along with the beef I had eaten, so my next step was to decide what to do about the food that remained out there on my plate. Did I dare try the Kobe again? No—those two bites were more than enough. But how would I justify not eating that last morsel, that forty-eight-dollars-worth of succulence?

I composed myself and returned to the table.

Jim looked up as I approached. "Are you alright?" Then without waiting for an answer he smiled sheepishly and added, "I ate the last piece."

Vending machine, Japanese-style

HOW TO KNOW YOU ARE IN JAPAN

Tania Romanov

If beds are hard and cold, and toilet seats are soft and warm.
If breakfast looks like pickled cocktail party snacks that would
go well with sake.
If everyone bows fifteen degrees when they approach you, and
thirty if you seem important.
If there's a vending machine every hundred meters with both
cold and hot bottled drinks.
If public restrooms have many indented holes and only one
recognizable toilet, and that toilet is the only thing with
instructions for use posted above it.
If there's a 7-Eleven on every corner, but you recognize none
of the goods inside.
If gardeners trim the lawn with manicure scissors.
If everyone on the escalator hugs the left side … unless you are
in Kyoto, where everyone hugs the right side.
If manhole covers are works of art.
If girls take tiny, pigeon-toed steps while smiling innocently.
If you are feeling very tall but are only 5'4".
If toilet lids rise in welcome as you approach, you are definitely
in Japan.

Japanese pagoda, a tower of tradition

MEETING OF THE MINDS
Joanna Biggar

In the late 1970s, while living in Ghana, I met a couple, both fellow-Americans roughly my age, who were traveling around West Africa plying their trade as family therapists. We became fast friends and enjoyed discussing our fascination and love for two separate yet related countries: China and Japan. After our Ghana years, I remember visiting them in their house in Cambridge, often talking about the pivotal influence China had on Japan during the Tang (618-907) and Song (960-1279) Dynasties, a Golden Age for China. In particular, during the Tang period, much of Chinese culture—art, architecture, poetry, fashion and religion—found a new home in Japan. Think kimonos, stylized wigs, pagodas, landscape painting, haiku and Zen Buddhism, for instance. Although China moved on, many of these ancient forms remain embedded in Japan. It is said, for example, to see a representative Chinese city of the Tang period, visit Kyoto. So, when in the 1980s, then with two young children in tow, Cathy and David went to practice family therapy in Kyoto for two years, I was not surprised but highly intrigued.

They lived in a small house in an upper-middle-class neighborhood, near the Aoibashi Clinic, where they worked. They

57

learned to unroll their futon, or bedding, over the tatami reed floor mats and to draw shut their paper sliding doors. They delighted in the three-foot-deep family-style bath and especially in the small interior garden with its maple tree, red berries and fountain. But they also enjoyed their Western-style bunk beds, desks and eat-in kitchen with refrigerator, stove and cupboards. They experienced a warm welcome in Kyoto, from the marvelous kindergarten teachers who felt responsible for the well-being of their two children to the neighbors who lent a hand with household repairs and offered snacks of octopus and Scotch. But they confessed, the sense of being gaijin, or foreigners, never vanished.

Cathy recalled the time David was seen in the kitchen by a Japanese visitor. "She'd come to pick up her son and saw David by the stove. She began staring—a very impolite, very un-Japanese thing to do—but she was transfixed by the sight of a man working in the kitchen, which is utterly a woman's domain. To her, he could have been a Martian."

But it was at the clinic where the two were employed that the differences and the possibilities for a workable blending of the two cultures were most in evidence. There, in a playroom outfitted with a one-way mirror, the theories from a culture that stresses individuality, independence, directness and verbal expression met a culture that values group identity, deference to authority, indirectness and intuition. One of the main lessons, both Cathy and David agreed, that they took from their Japanese experience was the primacy of the group. They found that for a therapist, the most important word was *amae*, a concept of love and dependency at the root of Japanese relationships. Takeo Doi, a leading Japanese psychiatrist who had spent years refining its meaning, defined *amae* as dependence and the presumption of another's love. For an adult, the task is to find a more mature form of dependence on the family group, but not independence from it. According to David, strong dependent ties within a group curiously work against group therapy as an effective practice, because once the Japanese become part of a group, they have difficulty leaving it. But since a family is a ready-made group to which one has a lifetime commitment, family therapy is a useful tool in Japan.

Cathy explained how the uses of space and indirectness in the spoken language also have direct application in family therapy. "Empty space has a special meaning, a spiritual meaning. Japanese art has its power by virtue of what it doesn't show, and speech by what isn't said. In the middle of the everyday bustle of shopping, I would see a scene as simple as women bending over, selecting pickles. Something about the way they moved, the treatment of the space between them, the esthetic quality of the tableau they created would hit me—there's nothing like this in the West."

"Japanese is other-centered rather than I-centered," David added. "While speaking, the first-person pronoun is rarely used, and it's common to leave one's meaning inconclusive—at least to the end of the sentence, depending on what the listener's ex-pectation might be." In therapy, this can be a problem. "However," he went on, "sometimes the Western method of direct questioning has advantages. Avoiding conflict and assuming rather than verbalizing can be exaggerated to the point where contact is lost."

But sometimes, speech wouldn't work at all. That's when David and Cathy and their Japanese co-therapists resorted to methods rarely used in the West. "Doubling," for example, in which one person stands by another and speaks in the other's presumed voice, like a player in a Kabuki drama, could be effective. So could "sculpting," taking advantage of the Japanese sense of space, in which family members physically arrange and rearrange each other to show the relationships between them.

As it turned out, learning some of the crucial and fascinating differences between the "opposite" mindsets was key in finding solutions for many of the issues that were troubling people who came to the clinic. For example, one family that had recently returned after six years in Germany, where the father worked as a business executive, encountered a kind of shunning from their community. They were treated as tainted, foreign and no longer able to fit in, and their reentry was complicated by a most common issue—school refusal. They'd returned so that their son could enroll in a good Japanese school. But he refused to go.

The family had reached an impasse. To make matters worse, only the parents came to sessions, and since they had returned to Japan for the son's schooling, the boy's father was angry. Further therapy revealed that the father had felt undervalued by his bosses both in Germany and Japan and had become quite critical of everyone in his family, including his wife and daughter. His wife eventually spoke out—a difficult task for a Japanese woman used to deference to her husband. She lamented his constant criticism and called her husband to account for some of the problems. However, she too was part of the problem. She had limited her husband's access to the family, ostensibly to protect them. What these issues gradually revealed was that this family had to reach beyond traditional boundaries, share difficulties and communicate. In the end, the boy was able to admit his vulnerability and isolation, and the family agreed that he could apply to a different school than the one the parents had chosen, a solution that allowed everyone to save face.

Saving face was often critical to finding a satisfactory exit from therapy, Cathy explained as she went on to share a story of another client family, prominent silk traders in Osaka for generations. Their issue was also one of school refusal—their thirteen-year-old daughter was spending her days hiding under a *kotatsu*, a heating table covered by a quilt. But this family also represented another problem: the transition from traditional three-generation house-holds into modern ones. In their case, the mother was in constant conflict with her domineering mother-in-law, whom she felt was always supported by her husband. In earlier times, a young wife was expected to be completely subordinate to her husband. If the situation proved intolerable to the bride, she brought her own solution: a dagger to plunge into her breast.

Many years before, the daughter-in-law had tried fleeing back to her own family, but such a return brought shame, and she was returned to her husband. Presently, the family crisis centered on the daughter, and her grandmother had tried traditional remedies, which included tea leaves and consulting a Shinto priest. At the clinic, first the distraught mother, then the father, consulted alone several times with the Japanese therapist, who discovered a potent family secret—that the grandmother was not really a biological mother, but a stepmother. She came into the family because the father's real mother had died of tuberculosis, an unmentionable disease. The stepmother, who claimed lineage from samurai, stepped in to bring the family through the harsh days of WWII, and the poverty and disease that followed.

Cathy joined in the sessions when they brought the parents and two daughters in together. Two eventful things happened. First, the father revealed the family secret about the grandmother. Then the grandmother came in once herself. "She was theatrical and self-serving," Cathy said, "and when she left, an extraordinary thing happened. The father laughed at her, saying she was too dramatic." The family saw him in a different light for the first time.

While these breakthroughs were useful, the girl still refused to go to school. The therapists tried doubling, using an older sister to speak for her. But no definitive change happened, so they resorted to sculpting. When the youngest daughter's turn came to arrange the family, she put her family in a row together and her grandmother (played by a therapist) behind them. Then in a striking move, she put herself in front, confronting them all. This, Cathy said, "was a very bold action for a supposedly weak Japanese girl of thirteen.

"I then turned to the father and asked him how he would like the family to be. He reached out to the youngest daughter and asked her to join them, to sit beside her mother and sister. When she allowed herself to be brought in, we were very moved. The only further rearrangement was made by the girl herself; she wanted the grandmother to be brought in closer and for her parents to sit side by side."

When Cathy and David returned to the United States, I spent many hours hearing their richly layered stories. On the one side, they were stories of therapy and the disparate approaches to treating families in distress. But at the same time, they were the narratives of an American family trying to adjust to a deceptively different culture. As Cathy put it, since Japan is highly evolved materially, you think you are going to understand it, to fit in. "But," she said, "you don't. All the clues for familiarity don't lead to familiarity."

In the end, both Cathy and David agreed that their personal lives and practices at home had benefitted from what they learned in Japan. "In our society," David said, "we're so used to talking in ways

MEETING OF THE MINDS — JOANNA BIGGAR

that emphasize our separateness. To live in Japan is to learn about empathy and really joining other people in their world."

Cathy spoke of the wonder of things unexpressed. "If I met you here, I'd want to know about you, your work, your kids. But if we were Japanese, we'd want to find out how to enter a space together. We might talk about how beautiful the temple is in moonlight. Do you know, we got a postcard from our landlord showing a full moon. All he said was, 'The moon touched the blossoms,' and he signed his name."

Atomic Bomb Dome near Hiroshima's Peace Memorial Park

PEACE AND WAR

Tom Harrell

I never feel particularly tall—even though at 5'11" I'm taller than seventy-five percent of American men. And in Japan I was never conscious of my height even though I'm taller than ninety percent of Japanese men.

Still, it was hard not to feel conspicuous standing in a room of Japanese elementary school children. There in the Hiroshima Peace Museum, all eyes trained on an atomic bomb—and, I was sure, the one self-consciously giant American in the room. Thankful for the dim lighting, I nonetheless felt tall. Really tall. And guilty.

The bomb was not real, of course. The "bomb" was a ball about two feet in diameter, seemingly glowing in the darkened room, suspended over a diorama of Hiroshima the way it looked early on the morning of August 6, 1945. It was grossly, purposefully out of proportion to the diorama. The impending doom was palpable.

I wondered what the children were thinking ... was this a visceral, visual reminder of war's brutality? Or was it something from history books, a dutiful expedition, a box checked, information for a pending exam? As I would discover later, Japan's relationship to WWII is complicated, if not contradictory. But the message in Hiroshima is a simple and powerful one: War must be eradicated forever.

Hiroshima suffered an estimated 135,000 dead and injured in the atomic bombing and its aftermath. More people were killed and wounded in fire bombings in Europe, but the horror of such destruction from a single bomb has made Hiroshima, along with Nagasaki, synonymous with the terrible power of modern weapons of war.

I traveled to Hiroshima from Kyoto, where our group was staying for several days, by myself and deliberately so. This was a journey I wanted to experience alone, and mostly in silence. Even if I had felt like talking, there were few foreigners in Peace Memorial Park that day. The park is designed for contemplation. The simple and powerful monuments throughout the grounds, and the green expanses, speak without words. Indeed, at times words seemed almost blasphemous.

The Peace Memorial Park opened in 1954, only nine years after Hiroshima was devastated. It is a mix of simple stone monuments, futuristic architecture and walking paths. The park is on an island where the Motoyasu River splits in two. Across the river is the Atomic Bomb Dome, the one building remaining after the bomb. You cannot go in; it is a twist of ruined masonry and steel topped by the iconic dome. All else was vaporized.

For me, the most moving area of the Peace Park was a deceptively gentle, green slope. This is the Atomic Bomb Memorial Burial Ground. In any other park, a slope like this would be a playground full of children and dogs, a setting for picnics in summer and sleds in winter. But here, it is the resting place—if such a word can be used—for the ashes of the thousands of men, women and children who could not be identified after the atomic explosion, or simply had no one to claim them.

Modern Hiroshima is not a pretty city, at least not the parts I saw walking from and to the train station. Standard restaurants, shops and 7-11s fill the blocky, low-rise buildings. There is little "architecture." It is a far cry from Kyoto, the ancient Imperial City of temples.

But how could I criticize a city rebuilt from ash and radioactive ruin when the necessities of trauma, homelessness and the simple need to make a living in post-war Japan privileged utility over aesthetics? Hiroshima reminded me of some European cities, flattened in WWII and rebuilt from rubble, cathedrals and cobblestones left to the lucky.

The very lack of adornment and history in its plain buildings— even though bustling and prosperous—was a fitting, if unintentional, complement to the Peace Park. The effects of war do not end with a treaty; they shape generations to follow in ways both predictable and unexpected. Peace is a moral imperative, for those alive now and those to come.

Three days later I was back in Tokyo, and I deliberately sought out what I thought of as the "anti-Peace Park," though of course this was my own conceit, not to mention a cultural assumption.

For many years, I had wanted to visit Yasukuni Shrine, a Shinto shrine not far from the Imperial Palace. Dedicated in June, 1869, by the Meiji Emperor, it was built to commemorate all Japanese who died in service of the empire. The names, origins and birth-places of 2,466,532 men, women and children are recorded, as well some animals including horses and dogs (statues of animals can be found on the adjacent museum grounds along with those of soldiers).

Controversy erupted when, in 1978, the Shrine added the souls of fourteen "Class A" war criminals. The souls of over 1,000 war criminals, convicted by the Allies after WWII, were already included in the Yasukuni Shrine, but these fourteen had been convicted of "Crimes Against Peace," the worst possible war crime and a determination of systemic policies of cruelty and brutality. China and Korea (North and South), and other Asian countries that suffered from Japanese aggression, and under Japanese occupation, were outraged. The Shrine became a symbol of Japanese avoidance of war guilt, unapologetic imperialism, and of revisionist history largely absolving Japan of responsibility for WWII and atrocities committed by the Japanese.

The Shrine itself is similar to other Shinto shrines, and is set in a spacious, leafy park. By itself, you would never guess its controversial history. But nearby sits the Yushukan Museum, a military museum opened in 1881and rebuilt several times, most recently in 2002. Set in a modern three-story building, the Yushukan could exist in any American city. The displays are what you would expect to find in a military museum: a mix of wall maps with arrows indicating attack and counterattack, vintage photos, historic documents, uniforms, guns, a full-size Zero fighter plane, a tank and a submarine. At the conclusion of one tour I overheard one man ask his guide, "Why did Japan start WWII?" The guide's look of surprise was priceless.

As I walked through the museum, though, I could not help but feel disoriented. The explanations were not what we learned; indeed, they were often the opposite. The "Great Pacific War" was forced upon Japan by the American oil embargo declared in August, 1941 (which is an improvement; until recently the museum claimed the United States tricked Japan into war as a way to exit the Depression). The museum was a defense of nationalism and justification of imperialism. Korea welcomed Japanese colonization; Manchuria in 1931 "invited" the Japanese army to "restore order"; the Massacre of Nanjing was a mere "incident"; and Japanese troops behaved with admirable discipline. Only unfortunate circumstances prevented a Japanese victory.

Most striking of all was the last display, which filled two rooms with wall-to-wall small, framed black-and-white photographs, each about four inches square, all showing the faces of thousands of young Japanese men. There were also letters home, many exhorting their parents to "respect the Emperor."

Only after walking through the exhibit did I realize these young men were kamikaze pilots, some of the 5,843 Japanese men who died in suicide attacks. "Kamikaze" literally means "divine wind" and refers to a typhoon that scattered a Mongol invasion fleet in 1281. These letters were pilots' last words; no regret was apparent, only pride and sacrifice. I felt a surge of pity for so many wasted deaths; after all, the kamikazes did not prevent defeat.

But then I thought about the young American soldiers who were their targets, half a world away from home. How many of them died in these attacks? The same tender age, or younger, but with no opportunity to write a last letter—at least not knowingly. Waste upon waste.

Many military museums acknowledge the costs of war, even as they implicitly (or explicitly) praise sacrifice and individual acts of courage. The Yushukan makes no effort to pay even lip service to the horror of war—emphasizing only the shame of defeat. Fighting and dying for the Emperor, who was divine and embodied Japan, was necessary, even sacred. Peace was achieved through force and was useful only if it provided advantages. Peace, itself, was not a value.

The Yushukan was a discouraging experience. It was built long before "fake news" and "false facts" became depressingly ordinary phrases, but seemed to embody the scourge of deliberate misinterpretation and outright fabrication. Of course, in our own battles over American history and its interpretation I see echoes of the Yushukan. Who gets to claim history?

The Hiroshima Memorial Peace Park was depressing, too, but also achingly hopeful. It tells a story of forgiveness, or better yet of making no claim on history other than its existence. Its truth does not need varnish.

And in a hopeful way, both the Hiroshima Memorial Peace Park and the Yusukuni Shrine share as a common value a reverence for souls. Whether buried in a mass grave, or noted with exacting detail, the souls of the dead should be remembered. Perhaps the more we value the souls, the more we will respect the flesh and blood that holds them.

Hazmat-suited workers in Fukushima

Containment
(For the Fukushima Fifty)
Linda Watanabe McFerrin

Man in white—Hazmat/Level A—
ghostlike, moving, breathing slowly—
in my horrified dream I hear your ragged
inhalation-exhalation through the
self-contained breathing apparatus (SCBA)
they say will keep you safe
from radiation: particles and gas.

These could choke you, stop your already
laborious progress through a plant men made
to fuel a lust for power.

You are anonymous, face encapsulated
by the hood, voice rattled
by the supplied air respirator, pushed
into the voice-operated channel—your
umbilicus to clean-up operations.

You are my zombie hero, dead man walking,
while the Big Brains meet and find new ways
to slice and dice the acceptable margin
for terror.

If I could shower you in flowers, make whole
the body that you sacrifice, through some
bright communal magic, I would do it.
But you are that magic; you are the white-bright
light of courage that dares to contend with
the murderous pissing poison, the greed, the desire,
and patiently clean
it up.

Woodblock print from the series "Thirty-six Views of Mount Fuji"
by Katsushika Hokusai

BREAKFAST AT LAKE HAKONE
Ethel Mussen

FLASHBACK: December 8, 1941

We were at war with Japan. Pearl Harbor had activated a more detailed Western Defense Command in downtown Los Angeles. Each branch of the military enlarged its communication facility. Marine, Bomber, Fighter and Coast Artillery offices had a place around the Operations Board map of the region and every officer had a separate phone line to the outpost it commanded. Tension was high as the coastal area was guarded against submarine and possible air attacks.

A call went out to the business community, requesting volunteer stenographic help. "We need women who take rapid shorthand to cover incoming telephone conversation." I and two of my friends who also worked downtown volunteered for the shifts after work hours. The job was an amusing quirk on contemporary engineering. The recorders used to record the phone calls were new German machines that used sensitized wire spools to replace the older Edison-style flat records. They recorded well, but in the process of rewinding to hear a specific call, the spool sped back rapidly and tangled tie wire and often involved more than one call. We stenographers were needed to note specific call data to track and recognize the recording as the wire was disentangled. Our job was not perfect transcription but help in retrieving the actual voices in conversation.

We felt our service aided the war effort and, in the process, we became part of the military defense team, even though the reason was a mechanical defect. As the war continued, we found other ways to serve. I became a student nurse, worked some years in medical research, and eventually found a career in Speech and Hearing Disorders.

FAST FORWARD:

In 1951, my choice of careers took me to graduate school at Ohio State University in Columbus, Ohio. There I met and eventually married professor of psychology Paul Mussen. His field of interest was child development, and when we met he was already working on a textbook in collaboration with a college classmate. Completion took several years, but their updated entry in the field became a popular and academic success worldwide. The volume was translated into several languages by other professors, and Paul was invited to visit and speak at conferences and many universities. I often traveled with him and was able to enjoy experiences my own career would not have afforded, although I was well respected among my American peers. Paul wrote two other estimable books, so his reputation and invitations continued for a number of years.

So it was that we were invited to Japan in 1980. Our hosts were two professors who had translated Paul's first volume. They met us at the airport and took us to a fine hotel in Tokyo. Later we met their wives and were entertained in their apartments, and general plans were made for sightseeing in the city. "We have another surprise for you," they revealed. "Mr. Masaru Ibuka—one of the founders of Sony—has a major interest in child development. He believes that fetuses hear their mothers speaking in utero and are born ready to learn to speak. He's sponsoring a conference at Lake Hakone where he has a summer home and would like to have you attend."

So, two days later we found ourselves in a Cadillac limousine, marveling at the views of Mount Fuji as we neared Ashinoku Lake, also known as Lake Hakone, the crater lake that lies on one wall of the caldera formed by Mount Hakone. Once a summer getaway for Japan's imperial family located on the Old Tōkaidō Road, the area is filled with hot springs, historical sites and welcoming *ryokans*.

We, however, would not be staying in rented rooms. We were to be guests of the Ibuka family. Mr. Ibuka was warm and gracious and already revising our post-conference sightseeing plan. His wife was at their home—a comfortable house not far from the ryokans and hotels that bordered the lake. This clearly was a popular tourist venue. The conference attendees verified our impression.

The house we stayed in confirmed the status of Mr. Ibuka. A stylish yet traditional one-story structure with a surprising amount of floor space for a Japanese home, it featured outstanding views of Lake Hakone, its cobalt-blue waters ringed with verdant hills. There was a small video camera in every room. Our Japanese hosts slept on futon mattresses in their bedrooms. Foreign guests like us were furnished with Western-style beds. Bathroom facilities consisted of modern Japanese Toto toilets off a small hall leading to the large *ofuro* and pool. It was the best of two worlds. We'd have our breakfasts together with Mr. Ibuka and his family at a low *chabudai*-style table, sitting on *zabuton* cushions on the tatami. On one of the few times that Mr. Ibuka and I were alone having a quiet breakfast together, I felt familiar enough to pose daring questions.

"Mr. Ibuka," I asked timidly, "how did you happen to select American Cadillacs for your personal cars?"

"Oh, that's because I didn't want a Mercedes, and I couldn't pick a Japanese car. No matter which one I liked, it would have offended the other automakers—and they're all my friends!"

We both laughed a little and resumed sipping our tea. "Mr. Ibuka," I began again, "what did you do during the War?" and I sucked in my breath, fearing I'd gone too far.

He answered readily, without embarrassment. "I was a Communications Officer at an Operations Center." He shook his head with a wry smile. "It was those terrible new wire recorders we had to deal with. They drove me crazy! I knew there had to be a better way, so I experimented and worked out a recording tape that could be wound and rewound smoothly and still make a good recording. And … that was the start of Sony!"

I gasped and laughed in amazement. "You couldn't have told that to a more understanding person," I roared. I told him about my job sorting out messages on those same German wire spool recorders back in 1941 and what a trial they were for our team.

We had a laugh about how much we actually had in common—two people from opposite sides of an ocean, a war, finding a common thread leading them both into the world's future.

Calligraphy practice page at Henjoson'in Temple

NUN FOR A DAY:
WANDERING IN KOYASAN

MJ Pramik

At two thirty in the morning I sprinted to the two glowing vending machines I'd spied upon our arrival earlier that day. One humming behemoth offered chilled Asahi Extra Dry beer; the other, canned sake for three yen—three cents US. I pounded the sake button after plunking in three coins. I'd just escaped from my three asynchronously snoring roommates—think slamming pile drivers interspersed with full running buzz saws *inside* your bedroom. I gulped the cool brew. Bawdy laughter reverberated at the other end of the hall. *Make that two cans of sake*, I thought as I dropped in three more yen.

Thus began my two-night stay in Koyasan's Henjoson'in Temple in search of enlightenment. Raised Catholic, I'd tinkered with the idea of joining a nunnery when I was young and impressionable, and still wondered if I could ever live a monastic life, a life so far removed from my own. I imagined a Buddhist nun's practice to resemble that of a Catholic novice: a serene daily practice, chanting at sunrise, no emails, no demanding texts, no shopping, no Netflix—just quietude laced with a continuous, sonorous hum amid deep breaths of cool mountain air. But I may not have thought these images through; my journey had already required me to call upon unfamiliar rice-wine spirits on my path toward the sacred.

Chance had cast the Koyasan visit at my soon-to-be-sock-covered feet. My brief excursion in Japan included a two-night stay in the Henjoson'in Monastery, the birthplace of Shingon Buddhism, nestled among the southern highlands just south of Osaka. I yearned for a transcendent and transforming experience, ostensibly to build my karmic currency against petty touristic materialism and to experience a respite from my own harried life. I wanted what the quintessential reformed aesthete Oscar Wilde was rumored to have said: "To have no yesterday and no tomorrow. To forget time, to forgive life, to be at peace."

I arrived in Japan soon after a visit to rural Ohio. There, I'd visited with my Aunt Rose, so robust and spry at nearly ninety years, and the last living relative of my parents' generation. On the flight over the Pacific, I'd reviewed our jovial photos taken on her well-worn sofa. My port of entry, Tokyo, was the antithesis of the laconic, slow pace of eastern Ohio where I grew up. However, the gentle breezes surrounding Koyasan and its one quiet main street served as a strong reminder of home.

My pilgrimage to the Kii Mountains started with frantic subway hopping during Tokyo's rush hour. We next streamed onto the high-speed bullet train, the Tōhoku Shinkansen, speeding to Kyoto at two hundred miles per hour. Snatching the next express train to Hashimoto with four minutes to spare, we had a luxurious nine minutes to snag a third train for the final leg of the journey, the Koyasan cable car up to Mount Koya.

At the top of the incline, I strode out of the tram station into a white-furled mist that swirled around my shivering body. It was as if I'd just stepped into the gauzed cut of a film by Kurosawa. Muted winds whispered past my ears; fog fingers held my face. The air smelled phosphorescent. I inhaled the fresh scent of ancient cedar. The wind conversed with a garbled insouciance. I waited for the white-faced, toothless ghosts from *Ran*, Kurosawa's rendering of *King Lear*, to emerge at any moment as I searched for the front gate of Henjoson'in Temple, one of over a hundred temples that dot the mountain.

Atop Mount Koya we declined a taxi, deciding to idle toward the town as dusk settled. Signage was nearly nonexistent along the road; building numbers lit doorframes in kanji, indecipherable to me. Lugging minimalist baggage—what could a Buddhist nun possibly need for a two-day stay?—I wandered through the town past the roadway of the temple at least three times before several members of our group congregated at the main gate.

The massive wooden door of Henjoson'in welcomed us and a raked sand lawn hailed our entry. A genial monk greeted us in English, escorting our entourage into the monastery after first requesting that we remove shoes on the outer porch for the night. The rooms were dressed in traditional Japanese décor; tea sat hot and ready on the low table. Futons floated about the floor, each covered with an orange down comforter. The bathroom proffered a fine rectangular cedar tub, its deep, earthy scent inviting me to turn on the tap. I donned a robe and the two-toed white socks and zōri sandals every respectable monk and nun must wear, and my feet flapped to the central dining room.

Abruptly, a handsome temple monk appeared out of nowhere. Hand signals and anxious tones replaced civilized dialog. Another monk arrived and translated: I had committed *machigai*, the faux pas of wearing the kimono-that-must-remain-in-the-room. It was never to be worn to dinner. I scuttled back to the room to change. No operating instructions had accompanied the robes.

Back in our private dining hall, properly attired, sitting flat on the floor, I opened the box placed in front of me. An acetic scent stung my nasal passages. Lively oranges and bright greens suspended my appetite. Every meal served in Koyasan Buddhist monasteries is vegetarian, *shojin ryori*. Strong aromatic vegetables—such as garlic or onion—are anathema. Each supplicant received this deep red partitioned box with assorted non-meat items gaily presented. I did recognize the miso sloshing in the requisite lacquer bowl, as well as the reassuring white rice. Eventually, I ate everything—as any grateful nun would—even the briny orange rubbery substance that none of my fellow diners would touch. Rather chewy and salty, infused with vinegar, I swallowed hard, noting to avoid this dish if served again.

After dinner, all guests hurried off to rest on those glorious futons. A communal bath was offered, one for men, one for women. I gave in to a languid impulse and rode the disability chair up the stairway. I disembarked, but the chair stuck at the top of the landing, unable to descend. I motioned the problem to the tall young monk nearby. He promptly came over and kicked the recalcitrant device, and it wobbled back down its track. After surveying the crowded women's bath, I descended the stairs on my own two feet and had a soak in the private cedar tub.

Fully relaxed after the hot bath, I nestled between the floor futon and the bright ginger *kakefuton*. Darkness poured through the floor-to-ceiling windows. My suitemates settled themselves, eventually, into deep, loud snoring.

Back to the vending machines and my two a.m. meditation. I stared at the neon glow for twenty minutes. The monastery had quieted. Retracing my steps to my room, I listened outside the rattan panel. The inhabitants of this room had finally quieted, too. As I gazed into the darkness outside the window, a small rabbit appeared and skipped the grounds, later to enter my dreams appealing for peace and contentment.

Kappoonnngg! Raucous vibrations sped from my ears through my chest into the pit of my stomach. At five thirty that morning the temple gong boomed and we were spirited to the altar room and chanting hall. Three monks knelt with their backs to the visitors and began an intonation. They intensified their deep throaty song, their sutras soaring into a solid rocking rhythm. After an hour of sitting very still and reeling my mind back from its flight to the polished wooden rafters, the main monk, who wore the most colorful garb, turned and addressed the attendees. Bald and rotund, he smiled wider and wider. I only understood a few words of Japanese: *Arigato* meant "thank you" and *Koyasan* meant, well, Koyasan. But it was abundantly apparent that he welcomed all of us devotees, supplicants, and chanters, no matter why we sat with him and his two accompanists.

Through hand motions, deep kowtows, and wide smiles, we were instructed to follow a path down wooden steps into the monastery basement. Stepping on outlined stones, I followed the movements of every other tourist. Stop, bow at a rectangular glass jar, sidewise step. Repeat. We honored the clear glass boxes along the shelved wall. Hundreds lined it. They were filled to the brim with brown-gray powder and stones. I intuited, and later confirmed, these vessels held the ashes of departed monks— unnamed here, yet honored by countless visiting worshipers over hundreds of years.

Following this walk amongst the dead, many of us donated yen to the monastery to be permitted to copy Buddhist sutras by hand. Right to left, as instructed by the monks. I had read that *shakyo*— the meditative practice of handwriting sutras over and over— appears to counter dementia. With this in mind, I dutifully sat as a nun-in-training at the low table, filling in outlined kanji with a brush. Right to left, right to left. I had to fight the urge to start a new page, judging my efforts not perfect enough for the Buddha. My colleagues finished quickly; a young Japanese couple zipped through their page. For some confounded reason, this focused task slowed my usual quick response; after a time, I found myself alone at the table and in the room, encircled in silence. Sitting among the ashes of the monks, I pondered: *Why here, why now?* Why had my hand slackened in this monastic space?

The consciousness of death remains such an integral part of life in Japan. Even death's approach has produced a centuries-old tradition of death poems, *jisei*. A few years before this Japan visit, my son had honored my love of poetry by gifting me with a collection entitled *Japanese Death Poems*, most written by Zen monks and haiku poets. While I had wondered at his choice of anthologies (for Christmas? Really?), upon exploring the volume, the tradition of writing a farewell poem to life seemed cathartic and entirely natural. It is simply part of the continuum of dying that exists in Japan. Some Zen Buddhists believe a dead person does not enter a place of no return immediately upon dying, imagining their relative's spirit to hover on the border of eternity for decades, even centuries. This allows them to visit the gravesite and chat with the deceased, relating family happenings, emotional revelations, or even daily events.

As the ghosts of monks past surrounded me, my phone—which I'd been spiritually unable to part with that day—buzzed with a text from my cousin Jim. My dear Aunt Rose had been hospitalized and was not doing well. In the past week, she'd suffered health setbacks and discovered she had cancer. The vibrant woman I'd sat next to on the sofa just weeks earlier suddenly moved on a different path.

I set down the pen-brush and left my painted-in sutras on the table. Perfection at a single task such as this seemed an elusive ambition that truly did not matter in the infinite universe we inhabit. I climbed the planked stairs in search of a meditation.

Each day at Koyasan, the monks present morning offerings at six thirty a.m. for Kūkai (also known as Kōbō Daishi or "The Great Teacher of the Vast Karma"). Kūkai introduced Shingon Buddhism to Japan over fourteen hundred years ago. He spoke of three secret mysteries to his devotees: the secrets of the body, of speech, and of mind. Kūkai taught that the human body symbolizes the larger universe, reciting voiced mantras expresses the truths, and looking inward leads to a place of non-activity and peace.

Kūkai's followers believe his spirit continues to enjoy the vegetarian fare placed in a large, shrouded chest and ferried up to his mausoleum by monks wearing masks to conceal their faces. Visitors are welcomed to the daybreak ceremony.

The next morning, after the one-hour chanting and an unrecognizable breakfast, I myself walked toward Okunoin Cemetery, where Kūkai's mausoleum rests at the far end. To reach the wooden temple over his grave, I passed two hundred thousand grave markers of concrete, wood and metal sitting quietly amid soaring cedars. Stopping frequently to admire cloth decorations and corporate dedications on statues, I felt at home amongst these memorials to the dead.

As I approached Kūkai's resting place, another text jangled my cell phone. What would this new message impart to me here, halfway around the planet? Again, from cousin Jim: His mother, my Aunt Rose, had just died. As my footsteps halted at the base of the mausoleum, I relived my last visit with her. She had joked about politics, her health problems, the beauty of her garden. "She has no more pain. We are grateful," Jim signed off.

I felt blessed to be in Koyasan in the company of my dear aunt's global counterparts. As tears ran down my face, I wandered slowly, meditating on the deep spiritual moment of living the life of a Buddhist nun, if only for one day. I vowed that when I returned to Ohio I would visit Aunt Rose's grave and carry her the offerings of poppy-seed bread and pierogi, the Polish comfort foods of our clan. I would speak to her reverently, joyfully. She would relish an update on my travels and the profound and limitless nature of the world.

Japanese pizza, a favorite new tradition

Okonomiyaki—As You Like It

Laurie McAndish King

This pizza is alive, I realize, staring at it in shock. *And it's waving at me.*

I'm going to eat it anyway.

Hungry, tired and just a little bit cranky after a long day in a country where we don't speak the language, my husband, Jim, and I are in a tiny restaurant in Kyoto. Its specialty is *okonomiyaki*, or "Japanese pizza." Five small tables crowd together, and two other couples, both Japanese, eat in silence. Jim's stomach growls.

In front of us sits the pizza, steaming and sizzling on a small grill that's built into the tabletop. Chunks of shredded cabbage and other mysterious lumps jut out of the pizza's lightly browned surface, and there's no tomato sauce in sight. The aroma is hard to identify: Fried fish? Bacon and eggs? Pancakes?

Sprinkled on top of the pizza are thumbnail-sized semi-transparent shreds that look like flakes of skin. These stand as erect as arm-hairs on a winter day, swaying as if alive, waving at me from their plum-sauce pool, then melting and disappearing into the red, jammy surface like silent ghosts.

I am about to taste my first bite of okonomiyaki. Although this

"Japanese soul food" is served throughout the country, it doesn't really look like something I want to put in my mouth. We are trying it at the suggestion of our hotel concierge.

"Where do local people go for lunch?" we had asked.

"Kiyamachi … Japanese pizza. *Hai*," he replied. "Tasty and filling."

"Is it nearby?"

"*Hai,* nearby."

"How do we get there?"

"Between Kiyamachi-dori and Kawaramachi Sanjo," he directed. "Easy to find near kimono store."

Kiyamachi is a historic district known for restaurants, cherry blossoms and nightlife. Wood-fronted shops crowd along each side of a narrow, tree-lined river, and a graceful clump of bamboo or a small maple tree grows near each front door. At night, under an umbrella of stars, paper lanterns glow and the river sparkles with reflected light. We looked forward to a romantic walk to the restaurant.

And so we set out. But soon, two women dressed in green surgical scrubs with matching baseball caps approached, intruding on our intimate stroll. Each wore white gloves and a blue backpack, and carried a long grey tube in one hand. In the other hand each held a big white plastic bag bulging with unseen contents. As the women came closer, a low roar interrupted the peaceful evening.

"They seem to be wearing vacuum cleaners on their backs," Jim observed.

"You're right—they're actually *vacuuming* the streets."

"How often do you think they empty the bags?"

I didn't want to get into a conversation about housekeeping with him. These Japanese women were cleaning their streets much more meticulously than I had ever cleaned a carpet. Occasionally they pounced on a small piece of trash—a discarded straw or scrap of paper—and dropped it into their plastic bags. I ignored Jim's comment and suggested we move on.

After a little wandering we came upon a tiny restaurant next door to a used kimono shop—this had to be our spot! The storefront itself was barely ten feet wide, its tall window crowded with display plates of bright plastic food, bottles of sake and plum wine, and a big blue poster for Asahi Super Dry beer.

A shih tzu puppy with silky white fur poked its nose out the front door. Its ears were two-toned—rusty red and dark brown—and sported mismatched plastic barrettes: pink on its left ear, blue on the right.

I turned to Jim. "Do you think we should eat at a restaurant where the first thing we see is a dog?"

"Don't worry; they don't eat dogs in Japan."

"That isn't what I meant. What if it isn't *clean*?"

"The dog?"

"No. The restaurant."

"You're concerned about the cleanliness of Japanese restaurants?"

He was right—why worry? Everywhere we went in this country seemed meticulously clean, and we had just seen two of the reasons—the human street sweepers.

As I pondered our choice of restaurant, an American business-man appeared at the door. He wore an expensive suit and had apparently just finished dinner. A small spot of food adorned his red tie. I guess we still looked undecided because he addressed us.

"You like okonomiyaki?"

"Japanese pizza? We don't know yet."

"You'll like it. It's actually more like a pancake than a pizza. '*Yaki*' translates to 'grilled' and *okonomi* means 'as you like,' because you can order this dish with fish, pork, anything you like. Unless you're gluten-free. You're not gluten-free, are you?" He brushed an invisible flake of food off his jacket.

"No."

"It's made with wheat flour, starting back during World War II, when rice was in short supply. They fed it to the kids as a snack. The octopus okonomiyaki is a specialty around here."

"Is that what you recommend?"

"Only if you like octopus. I love it; get it every time I'm in town."

Octopus pancakes seemed unnecessarily adventuresome. *Maybe we should start off with chicken*, I thought as we entered the restaurant.

Inside, the elderly couple who ran the restaurant presided over a handful of small tables. Lean and rosy-cheeked, the male proprietor had a high forehead and perpetually raised eyebrows that looked like the wings of an elegant gray bird in flight. He wore a bright purple button-down shirt. The proprietress had a wide smile and an unusual, three-toned hair color: rusty red on top, dark brown at the roots and white at the temples—almost the exact same three colors as the puppy's coat, minus the barrettes, of course.

We sat at a small table with a rectangular iron griddle inset at the center. The Mrs. brought each of us a steaming white washcloth on a wooden tray, bowing as she placed them on the table. I wiped my hands, enjoying the moist heat and light scent, happy to be participating in a beautiful, time-honored tradition. Jim wiped his face.

"You can't wipe your face with that!" I whisper-hissed, upset at what was certainly a serious faux pas.

He looked bewildered. "I just did. And you don't need to whisper. They don't understand a thing we say."

Jim was right. The couple spoke no English, and we spoke no Japanese. It was going to be an evening of bowing and pantomime. Jim gestured toward the small hibachi grill in the center of our table. "It's just like Benihana's! There's a griddle in the middle. Hey, I made a poem. *Haaaaai-yah!*" He chopped at the air with his hands—his best imitation of a Benihana chef. The lady scurried over to our table, interpreting Jim's raised voice and odd chopping gesture as a request for service. I flushed with embarrassment.

"*Yōkoso. Konbanwa. Nanika otetsudai shimashou ka?*" she asked, bowing slightly.

We stared dumbly at her for a moment. Then I tried for any English she might understand. "Hello. Good afternoon. Good evening."

"*Nanika o nomimono wa ikagadesu ka?*"

"Hai? Yes?"

"*Menyū ga sukidesu ka?*"

"Hai." Clueless, I shrugged my shoulders.

When it became clear we couldn't order from a menu written in Japanese, the proprietress shuffled us out to the front window of the restaurant where we could point to plastic representations of the food we wanted. But what did we want? I couldn't remember the word "okonomiyaki," let alone pronounce it. "What do you think?" I asked Jim, eying the shiny plastic food. "That huge plate of cooked green leaves might be tasty."

"It's undoubtedly delicious," he agreed. "But not very Japanese-looking. We need something we can't get at home."

"That bowl of noodles looks Japanese."

"It's probably very tasty, but it looks like a bowl of juicy worms! I'm not eating that."

97

Then we saw the okonomiyaki, a pancake dolled up with a topping of dark plum sauce, squeeze-bottle zigzags of mayonnaise and a scattering of chopped scallions. This was the dish we had come for. We pointed, smiled and said, "Hai! Yes!"

The lady understood. She led us back inside where we sat at the table with its built-in propane-heated grill. She pointed at the grill, then put her palm near it and shook her head. We got the message: *The grill is hot; don't touch!*

Then she pantomimed that we would prepare the pancake ourselves. We had already successfully ordered a couple of Asahi Super Dry beers, but I wasn't optimistic about the rest of the evening. Which ingredients should we request—and how would we communicate our choices?

The beer had further dampened Jim's inhibitions—not that he had many to begin with—so he did the practical thing: tucked his hands into his armpits, waved his elbows up and down, and squawked like a chicken. *Baaaawck. Bawck-bawck-bawck.* It must have seemed like a safe bet; chicken sounds are pretty much the same in any language. But it didn't look safe. Jim is a big guy, and we were in a tiny space. I worried that his flapping elbows would crash into the woman at the next table.

Jim continued ordering. He put a finger to the front of his nose and pushed it upward, adding a couple of *squeee*-like sound effects.

I felt—and not for the first time—as though I were dining with a twelve-year-old boy. Surely the owners would kick us out at any moment. "So, we're getting the chicken and pork then?"

"Yes," Jim replied with a wink, "unless you want to figure out how to order the octopus. I don't have enough appendages for a request like that."

The proprietress covered her mouth with one hand and tittered, then bowed and hurried off. Maybe she *did* speak English after all. She returned a few minutes later with large stainless-steel bowls filled with batter, shredded cabbage, chopped chicken and chopped pork. Success! She motioned for me to add these ingredients to the batter myself. "Okonomi," she said.

"As you like it," I murmured, feeling like a fast learner as I spooned the cabbage and meats into the batter and stirred vigorously.

The woman's eyes widened in alarm. Clearly distressed, she reached out and actually grabbed the bowl from my hands. Time slowed down. I knew I'd done something terribly wrong—but what? And whatever it was, how could it possibly be more of a transgression than Jim's pantomimes?

The Mrs. waited until she had my full attention, then showed us how to gently fold the ingredients in, instead of beating them, and handed the bowl back to me.

"She trusts you now," Jim said encouragingly.

Thus instructed, I ladled batter onto the grill and the pizza sizzled for a few minutes. When it was brown on the bottom, our patient instructor flipped it with a wide spatula and brushed on thick plum sauce while the okonomiyaki finished cooking. When the bottom turned golden brown, she turned off the grill, sprinkled a large pinch of bonito flakes on top, and cut the pancake into six flat wedges, like a pizza.

This is when our food begins to wave at us.

"I know they eat a lot of raw food in Japan," says Jim, "but this thing looks like it's alive, and we have nothing to kill it with." He's right. The eerie little flakes of skin are nodding in the heat, waving *hello* … and I am going to eat them.

Without a fork or knife, we are forced to eat small bits of the pancake slices with chopsticks—not an easy task, but definitely worth the trouble. Our chicken-and-pork okonomiyaki is delicious: warm and savory, crispy on the outside, soft on the inside, and flavored with creamy mayonnaise, tart plum sauce and salty bonito flakes.

Jim points to the bonito flakes. "I think these are from a dead body."

This time I don't bother to scold him, finally realizing it really doesn't matter what he says. I also realize I *love* that about him—that, unlike me, he is far more interested in connecting and communicating than in worrying about whether he might look foolish. He's willing to take things in stride, whether it's an obsession with tidy streets, a dog in barrettes, or a pizza with a will of its own. Thanks to Jim, we have discovered a delicious dish—of soul food, no less—just "as we like it." And we are enjoying an evening with the delightful proprietors of this Japanese restaurant through pantomime, food and laughter.

Japan's beloved dog, the Akita

Hachiko and Me

Linda Watanabe McFerrin

It seemed appropriate to meet travel companion Tom at the Hachiko Memorial Statue just outside the Shibuya Station for our visit to the Love Hotels on Dogenzaka Hill. For what is Hachiko if not a testament to love ... although perhaps not the kind of love one finds in these provocatively decorated nests of iniquity. I'd wanted to investigate them ever since they'd become a setting in my dark and weirdly erotic novel, *Dead Love*. After all, I was in Tokyo with a group of travel writers and although it was a whirlwind of a trip, I'd found a small opening in my calendar. I decided to shoe-horn it in, one of my favorite ways to do things.

I'd been told by someone I thought was in the know that I couldn't actually "visit" one of these hotels without a "partner." Tom seemed the perfect choice for the role. Tom wasn't particularly enthusiastic although, like me, he confessed to being a bit curious since, like me, he'd never visited one. The hotel I'd described in my novel—the one frequented by the yakuza Ryu and Erin, the zombie—was just like other Love Hotels: a sexual getaway for strangers or frustrated couples stymied in their affections either by imagination, society, or by the limited space and therefore privacy in many Japanese dwellings. The hotels, which feature a décor that frequently ends in "ish"—think *garish, fetish*—have been popular since the seventeenth century. The amorous intentions of the people of Edo (old Tokyo) and Kyoto gave birth to them back then. I, however, had first become familiar with their like in modern day California where we settled after my Japanese grandmother died. My half-Japanese mother—Georgiana Mildred Mitsuko Watanabe Hughes—was crazy about San Luis Obispo's Madonna Inn. Its rooms—Caveman, Love Nest and Romance Suites, among others—appealed to her for all the same reasons her countrymen and women love Love Hotels. I guess my own fascination might have had something to do with a heredity that I cherish.

My plan was simple. Tom—who was not interested in mc at all—and I would rent a room for a "short stay" or *kyukei*, have a look around, and *then* … I would write about it. An online preview of the various offerings only whetted my appetite. I was like a child picking through a box of garishly decorated candies.

And so it was that one morning, having found a bit of room in my otherwise crammed itinerary, I grabbed the train to Shibuya Station. I invited Tom—who also had a very small hole in his schedule—to meet me very close to where the vast tide of Shibuya-destined passengers generally alight: the Hachiko Memorial Statue, not far from the station's Hachiko entrance.

When I arrived at Shibuya Station, it was bustling … but this station is always packed. There is a constant din in Shibuya: construction noise, traffic, the international chatter of voices, music, and the pulsing and perpetual bell-ringing-electrical-jingle-and-plink of pachinko. It's quite chaotic and a difficult place to meet up with someone unless you pre-select a café or a pachinko parlor or a Love Hotel. But the ideal, in fact the only workable meeting point as far as I was concerned, was the sweet little statue of Hachiko. So it was that as I stepped out of the station, I checked my location and headed immediately into the throng.

The story of Hachiko is a moving one. I have always loved dogs and admired them, as did everyone else in my immediate family, not just because they are adorable or because my parents were so fond of them, but because of what dogs embody. The devotion and sacrifice of these canine companions is legendary, and their expression of love and fidelity cuts to the very core of the Japanese ethos. I had first heard of Hachi or Hachiko from my mother, but to Japanese kids, the tale of Hachiko is as ubiquitous as American kids' tales about the Easter Bunny, although Hachiko's story is true. A farm-born Akita, one of the most popular dog breeds in Japan, Hachi was born in 1923 and adopted by Hidesaburo Ueno, a professor of agriculture who lived in Tokyo. Every workday Hachi and Ueno walked together to Shibuya Station where Ueno caught the train to his job at Tokyo University, and every day Hachi would greet him at the station when he returned. One day, however, Ueno did not come back. He had suffered a brain hemorrhage on the job. Hachiko waited and waited. He did so for nine years, his dedication touching the hearts of everyone in Shibuya and eventually in all of Japan. When he died, his body was placed in the National Science Museum in Tokyo, and a monument to him was erected next to Ueno's tomb in Aoyama cemetery. And today a statue of the dog whose devotion endured through death and time still stands watch at Shibuya Station.

I headed to that statue to begin *my* watch. It was easy to spot the monument. There stood Hachiko, waiting in bronze for all eternity in the center of an enormous crowd of tourists and locals lolling, voguing, snapping selfies. People there for their meetups did not have to wait long. Friends, family, lovers, emerged from the station or approached from the byways, found one another and moved on. Groups of school children and teens loitered with companions, laughing and socializing until they tired of their group vigils.

I began to feel an uncomfortable affinity with Hachiko. As I watched, I started to feel quite sorry for myself. The lure of the Love Hotels diminished. I was feeling something far more *kodoku*. I felt jilted, abandoned, a wallflower, a lonely heart, a loser. I had to wonder if Hachiko felt that way. *No,* I thought. *No. He was made of stronger stuff.*

I pondered this for a while before I started to make excuses. First for Tom: I couldn't reach him on his cell phone—he must have forgotten it, mislaid it, accidentally turned it off. Then, after what seemed like hours (although it was not actually quite that long) I began to realize that Tom wasn't coming. After all, our connection was nothing like Hachiko and Ueno's. Tom and I were mere travel companions. Good ones, I've always thought, but hardly what anyone could call devoted. And this little escapade was about Love Hotels, about quick, impermanent encounters, not the kind of fidelity that Hachiko embodied.

Thus, as I stood contemplating and going ever deeper into the meaning of my sad circumstance, it dawned on me that Tom wasn't coming. And although I was kind of enjoying my pitiable state, I was also, in fact, being quite silly. After all, there would be no grave for me in a cemetery. There'd be instead a short ride to the next station, Harajuku, and a walk down Takeshita-dori; maybe a restorative visit to Meiji Jingu, Tokyo's most famous Shinto shrine, where I could contemplate the nature of connection and all things that pass. That is my world anyway: a whirlpool of activity, temporality, impermanence.

I later found that Tom had forgotten or, more accurately, "blown off" our little rendezvous. It might be that, in the end, he found the prospect of ferreting out the mysteries of a Love Hotel with me daunting or ridiculous or both. I, for that matter, had certainly learned something about myself and about love, once again finding myself so very "Western" and "wanting" and "un-Japanese" … at least in that ancient, devoted, "Hachiko" way. Of course, unlike Hachiko, an Akita canine companion faithful to a beloved master, I didn't have as much skin in the game. In the end I was glad I had the good sense to leave. But I still feel significant admiration for Hachiko and a great deal of empathy … although I am so glad that I'm more like a cat or a snake … but that is another tale.

The author's new hamon

MY HAMON

Tania Romanov

Japan kept casting a spell on me, sending me things I didn't know I was seeking.

I was roaming about, exploring with no explicit purpose, but the country reached much deeper into me than I had expected. Perhaps that is the ultimate gift of a lifetime of travel: I am not desperately seeking to acquire either possessions or impressions, leaving me open to chance.

One of my companions, one-hundred-and-one-year-old Ethel, travels the world collecting fine pottery and was visiting a renowned expert in northern Kyoto. I planned to spend the morning walking and told her I would meet her at his studio. It was a few miles north from where we were staying, near the Silver Pavilion. Ginkaku-ji is another name for this Zen shrine at the end of the intriguingly named Philosopher's Trail, which winds along a small creek and through a number of temples. It sounded fascinating, and I couldn't resist heading there.

Saving the Philosopher's Trail for the return journey, I roamed generally northward, passing through neighborhoods of delicate pocket-sized gardens and homes where people still slept on tatami mats. I lingered at canals crossed by small "walking bridges" and overhung by willows. I watched women carrying translucent umbrellas—bodies constricted by narrow kimonos—delicately stepping their way across wet bridges that consisted of nothing more than twelve-inch-wide boards.

Three hours later I reached our meeting place—or the spot where it should have been. I stood in a dirt field beyond a dead-end road, at the edge of a cliff that had captivating views, but nothing resembling the studio I was seeking. In desperation I chased the only human being in sight, a slender dark-haired young man speeding down the road. When he realized I was too old to accost him, he paused, looked at the address and map on my phone, and shook his head. He was not familiar with that street. We had no common language, but at my silent urging he called the gallery and discussed its location with the owner. He then indicated I should follow him. Ten minutes and two phone calls later he pointed to the end of an alley where I saw someone waving in greeting. The enormous hug I gave him brought a big smile to his politely reserved face as we parted.

I was comforted to learn that taxis have the same problem as this walker did in finding the studio. I also realized that I had heard of the man who was waving me in just a few months earlier. Robert, it turned out, was the expert who had guided my London friends through the Japanese world of ceramics and helped them invest an unexpected windfall. While I wasn't looking to spend a small inheritance on sake cups and flasks, I enjoyed the beauty of the art, and Ethel explored his collection joyously and did buy a few pieces.

While my friend and I were roaming the gallery, Robert sat down on the floor and took out an instrument I had never seen before. From the moment he touched it I was captivated. It looked like the lower half of a giant black steel ostrich egg with a flat top that had zigzag openings. They were rough but had an inherent geometry, as if lightning had guided the maker's hand at the moment of its creation.

I have since learned that this instrument—a hamon—was created in the 1990s by Teppei Saitoh, a percussionist and sculptor, inspired by the sounds of a water bell in a temple garden and ancient slit drums. He only makes a few of these every year, each one lovingly formed and unique in size and sound.

Sachiko Nagata, a hamon performer, describes it this way, translated by her from Japanese to French and by me to English.

The Hamon and I

The hamon, instrument of essence, instrument of sound.
Article of metal holding nature close.
The simple beauty of its shape provides a sense of calm.
Just as a temple bell, each of its sounds evokes
a universe and penetrates people's hearts.
The sound of a small hamon evokes a fairy.
The sound of a large hamon evokes the earth.
Its resonances merge with the wind, the rain, the cry of an insect.
They are never in discord with the sounds of nature.
When I play the hamon, I merge into it and soar through
a world of impressions and distant memories.

— Sachiko Nagata (translated by Tania Romanov)

In Robert's studio, as a baton that looked like a rubber-tipped chopstick tapped the metal, I was transported to my redwood grove in California, where meditation gongs I had brought from Burma create a sacred temple. And then I moved past that memory and into understanding why those unknowable forces that watch over me had sent me, with my modest interest in fine pottery, to this particular gallery.

Robert handed me the batons and I reluctantly tapped. I love music and spent my childhood trying to master piano, and then singing; finally violin. My singing had to be confined to the shower as no one could bear listening to it. My loss of the second-to-last chair in the violin section of my high school orchestra confirmed my total lack of musical talent. But every tap on this hamon elicited a sound more beautiful than the previous, and they blended into each other, creating music—a personal composition that required no translation on its way deep into my essence.

I walked out of there the elated possessor of this divine gift.

The next day I called Robert to see if my other friends could come visit him to see and possibly acquire a hamon. He warned me that they would have to wait up to a year, for very few of these were available. He also admitted he should not have sold that particular hamon. My hamon. The one that would shortly be flying across the ocean to me in a custom wooden box. His wife, who kept the records, had intended my hamon for another order. I paused for a long time before speaking, close to tears as the words came out of my mouth, but felt I had no alternative.

"Would you like it back?"

A wave of regret hit me as I endured the pause that followed my words. I had no idea I was already so attached to this specific one, but I knew I would wait, however long it took. And that my hamon could not begin its new life through deception. I had to offer it up.

"I could not ask that of you."

A wave of relief greeted his words. I didn't offer it twice.

A few weeks later it was not a heavenly hand but the UPS delivery truck that brought a lightweight box made of pale wood, perhaps balsa. The Japanese have a delicate touch with packaging and this was no exception. I eagerly unwrapped the beautiful ribbon, read the inscription on the box, and admired Mount Fuji on the red seal.

Soon my hamon assumed a place of pride on a handcrafted table by a large window overlooking San Francisco Bay. It sits comfortably on its looped coil made from rough jute or sisal, akin to those that support water jugs on women's heads throughout rural Asia.

I often play my hamon as the sun sets over the beautifully glowing Golden Gate Bridge or when the fog rolls in, blanking the scene before my eyes, making me feel I have drifted into space. The sounds float with me, only improved by the fact that my favorite cocktail often accompanies the experience.

Japan is just beyond that bridge. Well, a few thousand miles beyond that bridge, but when I play and stare I see it.

I know it is out there
I know it is in here
Sharing my space
Sharing my life.

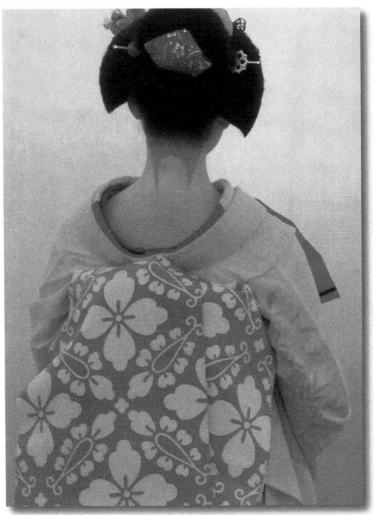

Japanese geisha in training

The Encounter

Michele Rivers

After landing in Tokyo, I spent my first few days in Japan following trails of blossoms. I was fulfilling my lifetime goal of seeing the spring cherry blossoms in all their glory. Late March in Tokyo is warm, so I walked to Ueno Park, where an estimated 800 cherry trees line the central pathway. The cherry blossom—or *sakura*—is the national flower of Japan. What shocked me at the time was the density of people. Under every tree families had spread out blankets or tarps to claim a picnic space. *Hanami*—flower viewing—is a favorite tradition in Japan, celebrating the arrival of spring with eating and drinking. Charming rows of shoes lined the edges of each picnic area. Between blankets, bodies, food and shoes, there was hardly an inch of unclaimed ground. The number of people gathered seemed incredible, so much so that I found it difficult to really appreciate the stunning trees above the celebratory masses. My fantasy of drifting through rows of cherry trees with pink blossoms gently falling onto my hair did not materialize. I went to another park where I was too late for the blossoms, as indicated by the lack of picnickers, the worn grass and the carpets of browning petals beneath the rows of cherry trees.

When I arrived in Kyoto, it was cooler, which meant I was a little early for the full bloom; the buds were still tight on many of the branches. Deciding to take a break from my cherry blossom quest, I began a walking adventure. With no destination in mind, following pathways and my intuition, I found myself in Gion, Kyoto's most famous geisha district, located around Shijo Avenue between Yasaka Shrine in the east and the Kamo River in the west. While exploring Hanami Lane, I discovered some of the most beautiful traditional Japanese architecture. The majority of Kyoto townhouses, *machiya*, built before the Meiji period, which began in 1868, usually have mezzanines with low ceilings. They include windows with vertical lattices set onto the mezzanine façade for ventilation. The windows of the homes and historic teahouses are covered with bamboo or wood blinds—*sudare*. It is easy to imagine—behind the privacy of the sudare—a geisha preparing herself for an evening of entertainment or quietly sipping jasmine tea. The *okiya* is a lodging house with which a real geisha is affiliated during her career.

Don't be fooled: Every geisha is not genuine. There are hundreds of fabricated versions created in many businesses in Kyoto, where ordinary girls are transformed daily in the practice known as *henshin*. Many imposters roam the streets and temples. Indeed, for a hefty fee, any woman or young girl can turn from a moth into a butterfly. First, the face and neck are covered in *oshiroi* makeup, white face paint. White, red and black are the only colors applied onto the face. Dramatic eyes and red lips dominate. Elaborate traditional wigs—*katsura*—are then positioned with the assistance of hairpins called *kanzashi*. Wrapped in stunning silk kimonos, the transformation of the chrysalis continues. Nike and Adidas tennis shoes are replaced with high sandals—*okobo*. Gingerly, the girls step toward collections of perfectly coordinated silk handbags, where they make selections to complete the facade. Hundreds of these butterflies flood the streets of Kyoto every day, gaining confidence with every admiring tourist. Giggling, they FaceTime and InstaChat at every sacred temple and Japanese landmark. However lovely these transformed beauties are—and some are impressive—they cannot replicate the matchless grace and beauty of a genuine geisha. The girls who pay for their transformation are not the dignified, exceptional, and now scarce, geisha.

Geisha trace their roots to eighteenth century Japan. In the 1920s and '30s an estimated 80,000 women were geisha. By 1970 they numbered 17,000 and today, there are fewer than 1,000. Only 273 geisha remain in Kyoto's Gion district. They are masters of the arts: painters, musicians, singers and highly skilled flower arrangers who also trained for years in the detailed crafting of the tea ceremony. They are consummate hostesses, each one an expert in the art of sophisticated conversation. As young trainees—*maiko*—they spend a minimum of five years practicing each of these arts.

The following day, I planned on heading back toward the Gion district, but I found myself distracted by a lovely shop. I stepped inside to take a peek at all the exquisite delights artfully arranged on low wooden counters.

That's when I saw her. She turned, and instantly I knew that I was in the presence of a real, living, national treasure—a supreme artist—an authentic geisha. Every fiber of my being knew that this lady standing before me was the rare jewel, the highly respected, genuine article—a real Kyoto geisha. She wore an elegant beige silk kimono, white collar and obi sash. Every hair was in place, every fold and pleat impeccable. Delicate, yet confident, she reached for an ornate tortoiseshell hair comb offered to her by the attentive assistant. It was as if she were performing a delicate traditional dance. She turned her head gracefully to catch her reflection in the mirror proffered by her helper behind the counter. No movement was hurried. I stood transfixed, mesmerized, watching her compare two combs held gently and carefully between her long fingers against her hair. It appeared as if she barely moved. For a moment in time, my voice abandoned me; my feet were glued to the marble tiles. I was held hostage by the vision of this extraordinary beauty in the high-end boutique, which offered makeup and accessories to patrons of the extravagant and glorious.

Lucidity returned slowly. Tentatively, I approached the counter. The fragrance of cherry blossoms, jasmine and sandalwood surrounded the geisha. After introducing myself, I asked permission to take her photo. A demure smile crept across her lips. First she nodded. Then she said, "Yes, you may." At that time, I was ignorant of Kyoto's police ruling, banning harassment of any of their precious *geiko*. We chatted, or more accurately, I asked her a few questions. She had recently graduated from maiko to geisha. She humbly but proudly shared that she was twenty-one. Maiko are between fifteen and twenty. She told me that she spoke five languages fluently. This woman was no maiko—meaning "half-jewel" or "dancing child." She had left the years of apprenticeship behind and was now a geiko. I soon discovered that in Kyoto, a modern geisha prefers to be called a geiko.

To say that I was in awe is an understatement. For a few moments, I felt as if I were in the presence of royalty, standing before a masterpiece or viewing a wonder of the world. I was entirely out of my element; I could not think clearly. I thanked her and mumbled something about my sincere admiration for her dedication to the arts and how honored I was to meet her. Later, I wondered why I hadn't invited her for tea or explained that I was also an artist and a writer. Why had I not told her how much I admired Japanese culture and design? In a bit of a trance, I left the boutique and found an empty bench in a nearby park where I sat for over an hour to review my experience. Indeed, I had not wanted to intrude upon the geisha's gentle ritual in the boutique; I didn't want to be another intrusive tourist. I wondered if she would have accepted an invitation to be interviewed. I regretted not sharing more with her.

My geisha will never know this simple truth: Although I was visiting her country for the springtime beauty of cherry blossoms, our brief encounter was as beautiful as their seasonal appearance. So sudden, so unexpected, it was, in fact, the highlight of my visit.

The Kamakura Buddha

LAND OF TEN THOUSAND BUDDHAS

Daphne Beyers

My journey to Japan began with a dream. I'm pretty sure it was a dream. A fox speaking to you isn't the sort of thing that happens when you are awake. At least not to me. Normally. Then again, nothing was normal after a twelve-hour flight that crossed the international dateline, causing me to lose an entire day. The jet lag wasn't as bad as I expected. In fact, I thought I was doing rather well … until the fox statue spoke.

We were visiting Fushimi Inari Taisha on the high, holy mountain of Inari in southern Kyoto. Ten thousand vermilion torii gates covered the winding path up the mountain, making me feel as if I were walking through a tunnel. Along the way I passed several smaller stone shrines filled with fox statues. Foxes are celebrated as messengers for Inari, the god of business and agricultural prosperity, but in Japanese folklore fox spirits have a darker legacy. They are tricksters not to be trifled with.

About halfway up the mountain, I stopped to rest in an alcove at one of the smaller shrines. Two stone foxes guarded the shrine. The one on the left held a scroll in its mouth. The one on the right seemed to grin at me with sharp, pointed teeth. I took a picture and then sat down on a cold, slightly damp stone bench, closing my eyes for just a moment. A voice spoke in English.

"That picture will cost you."

I jolted awake and looked around to see who was speaking, expecting to see one of my companions, but no one was there. A delicate mist had begun to seep into the shrine from the mountainside, chilling me. I had just decided to continue up the mountain when the voice spoke again.

"You will never leave Japan with that picture unless you answer me these questions three."

To my astonishment, the voice came from the fox statue, the one on the right with sharp, pointed teeth.

"Excuse me?" I said.

The stone fox grinned. "Three questions you must answer. Three riddles to unlock. Three gifts to appease those your photos mock. If you fail to placate the foxes, in Japan you will remain forever wandering in the mists, neither alive nor dead, but a ghost to the end of days."

The mist had thickened around me, shrouding all but the stone fox statue.

"You're not a talking fox," I said, my voice quavering. "I'm dreaming this. It's the jet lag and a bit of undigested fish."

I rubbed my belly, feeling queasy. It was true not all the Japanese cuisine we had eaten since arriving had agreed with me. Was I feverish? Fever can induce hallucinations. I felt my forehead, but it felt normal.

The fox statue stared at me, imperturbable as stone. Its sharp teeth glistened in the mist.

"Answer me these riddles three: Who is the Big Buddha? Who is the Buried Buddha? Who is the Boundless Buddha?"

"I have no idea!" I said. "There are thousands of Buddhas in Japan. A thousand in Kyoto alone. How am I to find just three? It is like searching for a needle in a pile of needles."

"None are in Kyoto," the fox spirit said. "That is your only hint."

"I'm only in Japan for a few more days. What if I don't find them before I have to leave?" I asked, thinking of my very expensive return trip ticket on Japan Airlines.

"You will not leave unless you answer my riddles and bring me three gifts, one from each," the fox responded.

"What gifts do you want?" I asked.

"Three pictures, of course. A photo of each riddle resolved. You can post them to my Instagram account."

I stood there flabbergasted with my mouth hanging open. What kind of fox spirit had an Instagram account? This was crazy.

"What if I just deleted your picture? That's what you're mad about, isn't it?" I pulled out my phone and started swiping through my most recent pictures. The photos of the fox statues weren't there.

Behind me, a woman called loudly in Japanese. She held up a flag and directed a large group of Japanese tourists into the shrine. I blinked. The mist was gone. The fox statues were stone again. The whole thing had been one weird dream, or maybe a waking reverie.

Still I felt uneasy. The idea of wandering in Japan as a ghost until the end of days wasn't something I wanted to take a chance on. But searching the land for a Big Buddha, a Buried Buddha, and a Boundless Buddha wasn't on my itinerary. I was traveling with a group and didn't have control over where we went. We were scheduled to be in Kyoto for a couple more days, but Kyoto was the one place where none of the Buddhas would be.

My phone buzzed in my hand. I had been added to a new

Instagram account called "Appeasement of the Fox Spirits." I clicked it open. A grinning red fox greeted me with a hungry glint in its eyes.

That night I searched the Internet for the three Buddhas. I figured the Big Buddha would be the easiest to find, and I was right. The Nara Temple complex was home to the biggest Buddha in Japan. That had to be the Big Buddha. But my searches for the Buried Buddha and the Boundless Buddha returned no useful results.

The next day, without explanation to my traveling companions —what was I going to tell them anyway?—I hopped a train to Nara. My first inclination was to rush to the temple and take a picture of the Big Buddha and then leave. I only had a few days to find the other two Buddhas, and I had no idea where to even begin looking. But Nara was too amazing to rush through.

Gentle deer roamed Nara Park surrounding Todai-ji Temple. The deer there have been protected for over five hundred years and have learned to approach people for rice cracker snacks. The deer willingly let people pet them, but they obviously don't enjoy it. They are still wild even after hundreds of years of living around humans who feed and protect them.

I bought some specially formulated rice crackers from a nearby vendor and was instantly mobbed by doe-eyed deer. Five or six hungry deer mouths plucked the rice crackers from my fingers in seconds. So much for my plan to hand out one cracker at a time to some grateful deer. After the crackers were gone the deer mob continued to stare at me expectantly. I showed them my empty palms. Instead of being dissuaded, the deer surrounded me and sniffed my pockets, back and front. A couple of Japanese girls giggled and took selfies with my deer-mugging as their backdrop.

Suddenly, the deer bolted. Another tourist had bought rice crackers from the vendor and was swarmed by my former mob. I quickly strode away before the deer returned for my wallet and passport. I followed a stream of about a thousand Japanese school children dressed in their smart school uniforms toward the massive Todai-ji Temple.

Todai-ji Temple is twelve stories tall and just as wide. It is built as a two-tiered pagoda-like structure with two curved golden horns rising from the top. I found out later the golden horns were actually golden fishtails placed there to protect the massive wooden structure from fire. The temple had burned down multiple times in its thousand-year history, but hasn't burned since the fishtails were installed. I pulled out my phone, set the camera to portrait mode, and headed inside to see the Big Buddha.

Two wrathful guardian statues with bulging muscles glared at me fiercely as I entered. They reminded me uncomfortably of the fox guardians that had sent me on this quest. I passed the wrathful duo and stood before the fifty-foot-tall Buddha of Nara. The colossal bronze statue sat in a meditative posture with the right hand raised in blessing and the left hand cupped in its lap. Its bronze had long ago oxidized to dark gray, almost black. I gaped at its immensity. Its ears alone were eight feet long. There was no way I would get the entire Buddha in my picture frame with my cell phone camera.

I stepped back and snapped a photo capturing the meditating Buddha's head and the right hand mudra. I hoped it would be good enough to appease the fox spirits. I snapped a bunch more pictures just in case.

Later at the hotel, while I was scrolling through my photos of the Big Buddha looking for the best one, I reflected on the absurdity of my predicament. What was I so worried about? The fox had clearly been a dream. Why was I taking its threats so seriously? It was the Instagram account, I decided. I could explain away a talking fox as a dream, but I didn't dream up an Instagram account. That was real.

There had to be a rational explanation. Maybe there was a device at the shrine that read people's Bluetooth connection on their cell phones and linked them to the Instagram account? The more I thought about it, the more sense it made. I was falling for a practical joke! I should go back to Fushimi Inari Taisha and hunt for the device. Except I had no time. We were leaving for Mount Koya in the morning. I decided that as practical jokes go, this one did no harm. It got me to see the Nara Buddha, which hadn't been on my original itinerary.

I opened the link for Appeasement of the Fox Spirits and posted my best photo of the Nara Buddha. A message popped up. It read:

> The Big Buddha is found with ease.
> The Buried Buddha you will never see.
> Find him you must before home you go.
> The Buried Buddha is both high and low.

The message vanished before I could take a screen shot. A chill ran up my spine. My rational explanation didn't account for this message. How could a Bluetooth-sniffing device know about the contents of my dream? The whole thing was making me doubt my sanity.

That night I stayed up way too late searching for any reference to a Buried Buddha in Japan. When my roommate's complaints turned to dire threats, I closed my phone and settled into a restless sleep with dreams about being hunted by foxes and buried alive.

The next day, bleary-eyed, I traveled with my group to Mount Koya. I had never heard of Mount Koya before. It is a region of mountains in the Wakayama Prefecture south of Osaka, and the headquarters of the Shingon sect of Japanese Buddhism. We took a train and then a cable car that went almost vertically up the mountain. We stayed in one of the local monasteries that provided accommodation to visitors. I don't know how strict the monks' lives are, but the monastery offered beer in vending machines. I wondered how many monks sneaked into the visitor area for a beer.

We slept on tatami mats, which were surprisingly comfortable even for a Westerner like myself. It was early fall, but that high up the mountain the temperature plummeted at night. The only warmth came from the bathroom's heated toilet seat. I guess the monks figured you could wrap up in blankets to sleep so only the naked bum while doing your business needed heating.

Having no idea why we were there or what there was to see, I read a brochure over breakfast. Mount Koya hosts Japan's largest cemetery. It surrounds Okunoin Temple, where the founder of Shingon Buddhism, Kobo Daishi, is buried. Believers come from all over Asia to make pilgrimage to the site where they believe Kobo Daishi rests in eternal meditation.

I stopped with my breakfast bean curd halfway to my lips. Could Kobo Daishi be the Buried Buddha? I grabbed my phone and searched. There seemed to be consensus that Kobo Daishi was fully enlightened and considered a bodhisattva rather than a buddha. That felt like a distinction without a difference. In general, Buddhist schools were reluctant to name anyone a buddha other than the historical Buddha. For my quest, I didn't think the difference mattered.

I then considered the clue given in the ending of the strange poem, "The Buried Buddha is both high and low." I'd figured the "low" part was a reference to being buried, but I couldn't see how someone buried could also be high. I thought high might be a reference to the Buddha's exalted state, but now I saw another meaning: Mount Koya was high in the mountains. Kobo Daishi had to be the Buried Buddha!

I rushed out without finishing my bean curd. No loss there. The trail through the cemetery was a mile long and filled with an estimated five hundred thousand graves. Anyone lucky enough or rich and powerful enough to get buried there is considered a shoo-in to meeting the prophesied Buddha of the Future. I was only interested in one Buddha right now, the Buried Buddha, but I slowed to a respectful pace through the cemetery.

The fall weather was perfect. Warm in the sunlight and cool in the shade of the tree-lined path. I passed thousands of Japanese tombstones shaped like columns or pagodas and engraved in kanji or sometimes Sanskrit. There were many statues of the Buddha along the way, both small and large, some with red kerchiefs and bibs. I never did find out what the kerchiefs meant. Maybe they kept the stone buddhas warm through the cold nights. I took a lot more photos. I knew I wouldn't get an actual photo of the Buried Buddha, since he was buried and therefore unseeable, but I thought a picture of Kobo Daishi's mausoleum would do the trick.

I crossed Gobyonohashi Bridge, which lead to Okunoin Temple and the mausoleum. On the far side of the bridge was a sign in kanji with a translation into English that said that beyond this point all photography was forbidden. Oh no! How was I to take a photo of the Buried Buddha?

I climbed up about a hundred steps and entered Okunoin Temple's Torodo Hall, the Hall of Lanterns. Hundreds of lanterns hung from the ceiling, casting flickering yellow light among dark shadows. A dozen monks sat before a large altar lit by the glow of all those lanterns and candles. The monks droned a mantra in a deep, resonant chant that looped continuously.

I followed a line of pilgrims and knelt before the altar. The chanting and the flickering candlelight seemed to hypnotize me. Pilgrims streamed in a row behind me, bowing to the altar and passing on. Others, who'd knelt for a time beside me, got up and joined the flow. I stayed, feeling like a rock in a strong current of light and sound. My body stayed still but my mind began to flow in a golden stream of light that didn't come from the candles. My thoughts floated away and disappeared in the current until only the golden stream remained, flowing in an uninterrupted effusion of light.

I don't know how long I sat there. Time had no meaning. It felt like one endless moment of spiritual bliss and perfection. I could believe Kobo Daishi was still there, alive in his mausoleum, deep in a thousand-year samadhi, bestowing on pilgrims and even people like me, his blessing. After a timeless time, I bowed and joined the line of pilgrims to exit the Hall of Lanterns.

Outside we approached Kobo Daishi's mausoleum. I have no memory of the mausoleum and no picture of it. I just remember a soft, almost clear white light, like the delicate petal of a lotus blossom floating on a still pool of water. The rushing stream of light seemed almost garish in comparison. Crystalline clarity, stillness and peace filled me.

I have no memory of leaving. Perhaps a part of me never did. About halfway back to the monastery, the world came back to my senses. It was like waking from a dream, except I think this was the dream and that other world of light and perfection was the real thing.

We left the next day, taking the cable car almost vertically downward and then a high-speed train to Tokyo. My phone buzzed in my pocket. The image of a red fox licking its chops lit up my screen. I had no photo of Kobo Daishi's mausoleum to appease the fox spirits. For some reason I wasn't worried. Some of the stillness and peace of Kobo Daishi stayed with me. I felt as if Kobo Daishi's blessing was more powerful than anything the trickster foxes could employ. But what if I was wrong? I decided if the fox spirits could trap me in Japan as a ghost forever, then I would return and sit in front of Kobo Daishi's mausoleum until the end of days. That wouldn't be so bad.

I was putting my phone away when my thumb accidentally opened a recent photo I had taken in the cemetery. It was a statue of Kobo Daishi dressed as a simple monk pilgrim. The statue winked at me. I blinked. The statue was stone again. I sat up straight. I had taken a photo of the Buried Buddha without realizing it. Almost reluctantly I posted the photo to the Appeasement of the Fox Spirits account. A part of me liked the idea of staying in Japan forever as a ghost. I'd only been able to see a handful of sights in the ten days I'd been there. There was so much more to see.

Then I thought about home and my little black Scottie dog waiting for me there. Dorothy got to bring Toto to the Land of Oz. I had to leave my Toto behind. Being a ghost would have its downsides. No food. No hugs. No furry warmth on a cold night. If I was ever to see my fuzzy companion again, I would have to find the last Buddha.

My screen lit up with an Instagram message. It read:

Two Buddhas you have found. The Fox Spirits are pleased. Discover the last Buddha to make them appeased.

Boundless is this Buddha no temple could contain.
Even should the heavens fall, this Buddha will remain.
Find the Boundless Buddha the Divine Winds set free.
Post this last photo and your debt paid, I'll decree.

I spent the rest of the train ride pondering who could be the Boundless Buddha. By the time we arrived in Tokyo, I knew. The next day, my last full day in Japan, I hopped a train to the seaside town of Kamakura, forty-five minutes from Tokyo.

Kamakura was the political center of Japan from the twelfth to fourteenth centuries. It was during this period that a local Buddhist priest raised funds to build a huge bronze statue of the Amida Buddha, the Buddha of Boundless Light. The Amida Buddha statue, known as the Kamakura Buddha, was the largest Buddha statue in Japan until the Nara Buddha statue was built a few centuries later. It was housed in an equally huge temple until the kamikaze, or divine winds, created a cyclone followed by a tsunami that destroyed it. Since then the Amida Buddha of Kamakura has sat in the open air.

I walked the tan, brick-paved streets of Kamakura toward the sea, passing a French bulldog and a calico cat lazing in the sun. One of the stores along the way displayed beer for sale with the Kamakura Buddha's face on the label. I entered the temple grounds. There, out in the open, unbounded by walls or roof, sat the Boundless Buddha.

Without a temple, the Kamakura Buddha seemed larger than the Big Buddha of Nara, even though I knew it was slightly smaller. Centuries of weather had turned the bronze a beautiful shade of sea green. The Buddha sat in the meditative pose of Amida with its neck bent slightly downward. Its hands rested in its lap, palms up, thumbs and fingers touching, forming a figure eight on its side or the mathematical sign of infinity. The giant Buddha seemed both intimidating and approachable at the same time.

I sat in the shade of a tree to the left of the Buddha and fell into contemplation. In the West, statues are admired for their artistry and history but they are just dead stone, relics of a bygone era, monuments of a past lost to time and progress. The Kamakura Buddha, though made of bronze and forged by mortal hands, was somehow alive. The statue glowed with an inner light, a light that transcended the world of the senses, that transcended even time itself. An eternal light unbroken by the prism of the mind.

Tourists came and went like waves lapping at the shore. The Boundless Buddha sat unperturbed, a deep ocean of meditation. The world's noises became the hum of a mantra. The flutter of leaves, a kaleidoscope of light and shadow, the yin and yang of perception. Behind it all, just out of reach, lay something enormous. Something unfathomable. A boundless reality that could not be encircled by my mind. I gave up trying. For one perfect moment life balanced as if on the head of a pin, and I beheld a world of wonder.

Needless to say, the fox spirits were appeased, and I returned home to write about my adventures in Japan. Yet I feel a part of me stayed behind, perhaps fulfilling my other destiny as a ghost. Not wandering Japan with an insatiable appetite, but drinking deeply of the waters of the three Buddhas.

Torii gates, the transition from mundane to sacred.

In Tokyo, Finding the Kami Way
Linda Watanabe McFerrin

Rainfall and the loud complaint of crows threaded through the silence that filled the tiny *haiden* or hall of worship at Ueno Toshogu Shrine. From somewhere on the tree-canopied walkways that circled the shrine grove, the chatter of women and laughter of children wafted in on the mist. More faintly still—almost inaudibly—autos made their whispery way over wet city streets. In the quiet of that Shinto shrine in the heart of Tokyo, the nearly 13 million people who inhabit the metropolis seemed to be little more than a dream.

No dream, my arrival in Tokyo had been very much a reality and a pleasant one: the gentle ministrations of the Japan Airlines staff, the clockwork arrival and efficiency of the airport shuttle that whisked me from Narita along the expressway, over the Rainbow Bridge and deposited me in what looked like Tomorrowland, the silvery sky-rise complex next to Odaiba Beach overlooking Tokyo Bay. I'd returned to Tokyo after decades of absence to see if I could find something that had eluded me in my childhood, some secret about this huge city in which I'd once felt so lost. That evening, lingering over a cocktail in the Sky Lounge of the elegant Meridien

Grand Pacific Hotel, I unfolded my city map to reveal the large splatters of green that indicate the city's many parks and gardens, squinting through the flicker of candlelight to find the little goal post icons that mark the Shinto shrines. In these shrines, or *jinja*, Japan's folk deities, the kami (both natural forces and humans are counted among their number), are believed to reside. It is said of the Japanese that they are Buddhist by belief, but Shinto by virtue of being, so in many ways these Shinto shrines house the spirit of Japan. I circled several, two of them in the Ginza, and refolded the map. On the other side of the moonlit waters, across Tokyo Bay, the sceptered shape of Tokyo Tower twinkled, the huge metropolis spread around it like an extravagant and glittering train.

The city of Tokyo covers more than 800 square miles, but on its vast system of interlocking train and subway lines, getting anywhere is only a matter of minutes and a couple of dollars. The next morning took me from Daiba Station (across the skywalk from the Meridien Grand Pacific) to Shimbashi Station on the monorail, a plush ten-minute ride past towers of glass and concrete. From there, a few more minutes got me to the Ginza, one of Tokyo's trendiest and most popular shopping districts. The Café Odiri, a lovely European-style watering hole at the foot of the Printemps department store, was a great place to get my bearings. Next thing I knew I was one of the butterfly crowd flitting from kimono shop to gallery to designer boutique as I made my way down Sotobori-dori. Carried away by material enticements, I almost drifted right past Ginza Hachikan Shrine. Situated on the first floor of an eight-story office building and not much larger than a closet, its diminutive dimensions came as something of a surprise. Missing were the cypress and pine that usually surround Shinto shrines. Nature's sanctity and man's harmonious coexistence with it are such an important part of the Shinto belief structure that its places of worship almost always incorporate some homage to this relationship. I wondered if the abstract paintings that filled the vitrines on one of the walls were supposed to fill that purpose.

Other features typical of Shinto shrines were compactly represented. A white-and-gray-clad Shinto priest, chanting solemnly to himself, manned a counter upon which wooden prayer tablets and other types of offerings for purchase were displayed. I bowed respectfully and watched as a young working woman in a cream-colored suit stepped in from the street, cleansed hands and mouth at a small stone fountain and positioned herself in front of the sanctuary. Looking very much like the raised entrance to a fine Japanese home with a place for offerings in front of it, this sanctuary, or *honden*, is where the kami is believed to reside. The young woman cast her coins into the offering box, rang the large bell rope to get the kami's attention, clapped her hands three times, bowed and clapped again. The ritual seemed perfunctory, a matter of habit. A few steps away the city rushed by.

Only a few of the shrines that I planned to visit were in the southeastern part of Tokyo. To visit Meiji-jingu, the capital's greatest shrine, I decided to take up residence toward the west, at the juncture of what were once Tokyo's most important roads. Even after Odaiba Beach and the Ginza, the fast-paced Shinjuku district, with its skyscrapers and towers, came as a bit of a shock. Entire cities exist within the walls of some of its 40- and 50-story edifices. Shinjuku Station is easily the busiest station in Tokyo. Over three million people pass through it each day. My dazed walks between business towers and fountains and past sex and cinema entertainments took me to Shinjuku Park and to beautiful Hanazono Shrine. Not far from Shinjuku, a short train ride on the Yamanote line, is Meiji Shrine, Tokyo's grandest, completed in 1920 in memory of Emperor Meiji, the ruler credited with the modernization of Japan, and his Empress. Only a two-minute walk from Harajuku Station, Meiji-jingu is impossible to miss, the 33-foot single cypress pillars and the 56-foot crossbeam of its monumental torii gate dwarfing everything around it. People streamed, looking small as ants, through it and down the wide walkways. Right behind the shrine complex, 133-acre Yoyogi Park was the perfect spot to sit and ponder the experience. Clouds of hydrangea floated in the patches of shade that framed stone picnic tables. Groups of students—young and old—practiced everything from violin to tai chi.

Regardless of the shrines, Shinjuku was wearing on me. I craved a quieter atmosphere. I knew just where to go. Packing my bag and taking subway and train once again, I headed northeast, toward Taito-ku, to a simple, but much-recommended, ryokan or traditional Japanese inn. The establishment's amiable proprietor greeted me warmly upon my arrival and took me upstairs to my room. Morning sun filtered in through the creamy rice-paper panes that screened the windows. On my bedding, a Japanese summer kimono or *yukata* waited, folded and pressed. On a low round table, tea cups, a teapot, hot water and green tea leaves promised a soothing respite. When I closed the door, the smell of freshly woven green tatami mats rose up around me. I studied the hand-drawn, hand-lettered map that the proprietor had given me. Umbrella shops, bookstores, bakeries, bathhouses, tatami makers, noodle shops, florists and a host of temples and shrines crowded the page. I'd found just what I wanted: a folksy, old-fashioned Tokyo neighborhood.

It was easy to rise early every morning, to drink my green tea and head out into the close-quartered maze of little businesses that made up my new environment. Nearby Nezu Shrine proved the perfect place to spend a sunny morning before lunching on *zaru* soba—cool, tri-colored buckwheat noodles—tempura and ice-cold sake. Another day, my backpack stuffed with goodies—little cakes with delicate swirls of sweet bean paste and golden *sembei* crackers in their sere, seaweed wrappers—from the neighborhood shops, I occupied long hours visiting shrines in the Asakusa district. The cramped streets of Asakusa, dense with merchants, are typical of Shitamachi, or the old downtown, when Edo—as 19th-century Tokyo was called—was the Shogun's power seat and the Shogun, not the Emperor, ruled Japan. I strolled along the Sumida River, watching the ferries cruise down toward Odaiba Beach, toward the "river gate" that had given Edo its name. In the evenings, I sampled the tasty and quite inexpensive fare of local restaurants and pubs and followed my gregarious landlord through the labyrinth of alleys, as he guided me past private shrines and cemeteries, telling me ghost stories, his wooden geta or sandals clicking before me as he led the way in the lamplight.

One rainy morning, I headed south along Shinobazu-dori, toward Shinobazu Pond, the Shitamachi Museum and the nest of temples, shrines and museums that dot Ueno Park. When I'd visited the park as a child it was only to go to the zoo. I remembered it as a great place for children, but it is a fine destination for people of any age. There, I stopped at Ueno Toshogu Shrine, stepped into the haiden and hesitated, stocking-footed, beneath the gold and cobalt portraits of warriors, princes and philosophers and listened to the rain.

I had been in Tokyo for nearly two weeks. A few days before leaving, I moved back to its center, to the Capitol Tokyu Hotel in Chiyoda-ku close to the Diet, the Japanese ministries and the parks and gardens that surround the Imperial Palace. A grand location and an entertaining one—Eric Clapton, Michael Jackson, Diana Ross and the Three Italian Tenors are just of few of the celebrity tenants who stayed there when in Tokyo—its ample rooms were quite a switch from my previous residence, and they carried a much higher price tag. Still, high prices seem in keeping with a Presidential Suite or an Imperial Suite with an unobstructed master bedroom view of Hie Shrine. My room, which was considerably smaller, also had a magnificent view. I looked straight down upon the koi pond where the fish, enormous torpedoes of silver and flame that looked huge even from my sixth-story perch, swam about in their languid circles.

Hie Shrine was right out in front of the hotel, separated from the street, like most holy places in Tokyo, by a steep flight of stairs. Inside its torii gate, it was peaceful, sunlight bouncing off the small gray stones of the courtyard. A couple of princely roosters, all amber and emerald, strutted about the grounds. I washed my hands and rinsed my mouth at the fountain, walked up to the sanctuary, rang the rope bell, and clapped to get the kami's attention. No longer hesitant, I gave my prayer of thanks, realizing at last, as I hadn't when I was a child, that the presence of the kami is delicate like most things of value in this world. It is found within a quiet heart, one that moves effortlessly from the frenzy of daily life to the silence of a Shinto shrine, in tranquility and a profound sense of balance, even in the midst of chaos.

Stone markers at Okunoin

ECHOES OF OKUNOIN

Tania Romanov

Every step took me deeper into the ancient heart of Okunoin, the largest and most revered cemetery in Japan—a shadowy forest of giant cedars and stone markers, of mists and mosses, of ghosts present and past. The trails, hidden under mud and needles, pulled me away from the well-maintained and heavily visited formal areas of pagodas and pavilions. Water dripped from overhead branches. Old stones leaned gently together. I slowed and followed a weak beam of sunlight to a mismatched pair of eroding markers, when a sudden vibration in my pocket interrupted my reverie. *Was someone trying to reach me?*

It was autumn and I was staying in a temple in the small mountain town of Koyasan, between visits to Tokyo and Kyoto. Previous travels in Japan, some years ago, had involved my high-tech business career. At that time, the polite, enigmatic silence I encountered made negotiation challenging. It hadn't started smoothly. One of the first executives I worked with casually mentioned that women walked two steps behind in his culture, a comment he came to regret when he learned I controlled his investment budget. His culture and I never matched wavelengths.

But now I wanted to see what it felt like to explore freely, to not worry about the next meeting or how to dress for dinner with high-level executives and geisha. My life had changed radically some twenty years ago when my husband Harold was diagnosed with an aggressive cancer. We both left successful business careers to appreciate days suddenly made incalculably more valuable than any possible financial gain. He successfully battled against all odds for sixteen years—almost half our time together—and we savored life even as the enemy stalked relentlessly.

But now he was gone and I dove into writing and photography and surrendered fully to my travel addiction. I was exploring different ways to see, and learning to appreciate the Zen aesthetic in my life and art. Surely a land where the *wabi-sabi* values of imperfection and naturalness were venerated had much to teach me. What I didn't know was whether I was open to learning from them.

I wasn't a natural for the subtle courtesies of Japan. My roots were close to the surface, as my immediate family had fled from Russia and the Balkans. My upbringing was raucous and combative; family members expressed themselves loudly and fervently. I worked hard to keep my sense of self, to not be overrun by their strong beliefs. I was outspoken and articulate; I shouted loudly and persistently. My writing is still more Tolstoy than Tanka, raw personal exposé rather than symbolic, measured haiku. But the pull of delicate Japanese brush painting has, after years of hard work, helped me create some of my favorite photographic images. And I have learned that even short sentences can sing.

I explored.

In Kyoto I walked the Philosopher's Trail along a creek bed, then veered onto side streets. I visited a pottery collector and, unexpectedly, found a unique instrument called the *hamon*. Made of rough cast iron and shaped like half a giant ostrich egg, this simple object, similar to a slit drum, converted my inexpert taps to tones as delicate as water drops in a hollow echoing cavern, a sound that spread like a ripple of water.

In Tokyo I roamed for days, confident in aimless exploration because my phone always knew where I was and where my hotel was. I walked through glossy department stores selling hundred-dollar mushrooms and marveled at the cleanliness of this city of millions.

And then several trains and a funicular brought me to the mountains, and to Koyasan. In the morning I explored temples of an austere intimacy that contrasted radically with the elaborate and vibrant Russian Orthodox cathedral of my youth. Instead of nearly explosive singing in many keys I heard modulated male voices chanting, their haunting tones escaping into the surrounding fog and forests. Memory and reality mixed and melded.

I stopped for a brief rest in my room and finished the newest mystery by Louise Penny, a favorite Canadian author. In the final sentences, the protagonist discovers that the name of his newest grandchild is Zora. My mother's name—and one rarely heard outside the Balkans. I pondered this as I moved on.

I walked on steep hillsides amid giant cedar trees that reminded me of the redwoods in northern California where Harold's ashes are scattered. And then I reached that moment briefly shattered by my phone vibrating.

It was my calendar. The first reminder, my wedding anniversary, made me laugh. We were so bad at dates that for almost thirty years in those days before smart devices it was my mother's phone call that first alerted us to the day's significance.

But there was a second reminder. Tomorrow, September 13, would mark the anniversary of my mother Zora's death. Suddenly everything about the day took on new significance. Harold and my mother had always been extremely close. My two loved ones were evidently tag-teaming from beyond this world to make sure I remembered them. I don't visit my family's graves, but here I was, in a cemetery, and they were using vibrating airwaves to communicate with me. *How very Zen*, I thought. An uncanny marriage of tradition and technology, of the sublime and the annoyingly pedestrian. Of my high-tech past melded onto my more contemplative present.

Rain turned to wispy tendrils of mist that wafted like the smoke from swinging incense burners at my parents' funerals. I stood before two stone markers—one short, one tall—one lit by the brief sun's glow, one in deep shadow. The pairing was perfect. My six-and-a-half-foot-tall husband towered over me as my father had over my tiny mother. I was in a perfect place, physically and spiritually, to receive and understand my mother's message. The very next grouping I saw held my whole family, everyone I had lost, represented by old stones covered with bright green moss, glowing in the dark, transcending temple and cathedral. I lost myself in that amazing mountain for hours, walking in silence while pilgrims and tourists passed on the lower trails.

I reflected back many years and remembered the continuing interchange with my hapless Japanese colleague. I was in my office when there was a gentle tap on the open door.

"Romanov-san," he said, bowing gently. "May I come in?"

"Of course," I replied.

"Romanov-san," he continued, with words that were unexpected and surely the result of some anguish. "I need to confess," and he paused, looking down at the floor rather than at me, "that my own daughter refuses to walk two steps behind."

It was his way of inviting me to his country, acknowledging that I—and my investment funding—would be welcome. It also spoke to the future.

I don't know how much Japan has changed over the last thirty years, in which his daughter has grown to middle age, and I have moved beyond that. The women I met indicated it was still hard to get ahead. But that's equally true in Silicon Valley. It is I who have learned to leave judgment a bit further behind, to listen to what isn't said, to appreciate the beauty in the subtle.

As a result, my experience of Japan was radically different on this trip from my previous travel. I was relaxed and able to deeply absorb a culture that was open to my exploration and easy to appreciate. I even saw the geisha as women expressing an ancient art rather than submissive servers of sake. It was in its new accessibility that Japan showed me who I was, whom I had become.

It was in Koyasan, as I moved in quiet contemplation, that my ancestors found me. They sent calm, rather than guilt over my lack of care for their gravesites or memory for dates. In that forest cemetery far from all our homes—past and present—my tears blessed their memories, and I walked for hours in a peace I have rarely found anywhere else, listening to them without fear that they would overwhelm my ability to think clearly.

Like baby Zora's arrival near the end of that mystery novel, life continually presents me with unexpected synchronicity and powerful signs. I no longer manage businesses or control investment budgets. The knowledge that we control little beyond ourselves has settled deep within me. My need to shout has moderated greatly, although I know it will never entirely disappear.

I reveled in my experience of Japan not because of how the country had changed, for it always held both complexity and subtlety. It was I—in the earlier chapters of my life—who saw the world mostly in black and white and was blinded by my need to transform it. It was definitely I who had changed. Who had learned.

To hear. To see. To just be.

"Cooling off at Shijo" from the woodcut series
"One Hundred Aspects of the Moon" by Yoshitoshi

Basho Replies to Li Po's Poem "Alone at Jing Ting Mountain"

Joanna Biggar

Dear Master,

Nearly one thousand years ago
you went to
the mountain and wrote
this poem:

Many birds have flown high,
Only a solitary cloud floats free.
Never tiring, we watch each other,
Jing Ting Mountain and I.
Only the mountain remains.

Across time and winds,
and the waves
of the East China Sea,
your verse has flown to me,
and
remained
in my heart.

At last, humbly, I reply:

Now she appears,
old woman weeping alone,
moon and companion.

For I know
what you will know:
that
the seer,
the seen,
and the moon
are one,

as you are with the mountain,
where
you wait
for us.

Li Po (701-762) was China's most famous poet of the Tang Dynasty. Matsuo Basho (1644-1694) was Japan's most renowned composer of haiku. Li Po translation by Joanna Biggar. Basho translation by Linda Watanabe McFerrin.

A mountain monk from *Saito Musashi-bo Benkei*

WHIRLING AND SWIRLING
ALONG THE WAY
Rob "Tor" Torkildson

It is a clear and crisp autumn day when I enter the wooden torii gate with a letter from poet Gary Snyder neatly folded in my pocket. I should mention that I had strong Buddhist leanings and had made forays into Zen under the influence of Dainin Katagiri Roshi and the poet Gary Snyder. One day a friend mentioned, mischievously, that I should look into the Yamabushi mountain monks of Japan. This led me to Snyder's essay, "Blue Mountains Constantly Walking," and my goal to find the mountain ascetics who practice walking meditation, own nothing, feel the entire universe is their temple and the great mountain ranges their worship halls. I soon learned that Gary Snyder was the first Westerner to become a novice Yamabushi (*sentachi*) and to be introduced to the mountain deities, Zao Gogen, and to Fudo Myo-O. Becoming a sentachi became my new quest.

An elderly monk in white robes sweeps the courtyard. The smell of incense and wild-herb-flavored udon soup wafts around and into my nose. The bulging eyes of a stone statue representing Fudo Myo-O scrutinize my approach. It is the first day of my training and initiation (*shugyō*) into the esoteric Shugendo sect of the Yamabushi. Beat writer Pierre Delattre once sent me to Nepal on a quest. His parting words ring like temple bells in my head. "Swirl with the swirl and whirl with the whirl, and no bones shall break."

Despite studying Japanese for four years, I am not ready for the esoteric language I am about to experience. Theirs is a language clouded in mystery and sacred mountain realms beyond my grasp. I will try my best to follow along. I will observe everything that goes on around me intensely and adapt. Hadn't I survived special-forces training in the military? Several priests wander across the courtyard with high-peaked hats and an air of authority. A muscular monk approaches me, and I hand him my approval from the head priest, Kokuji, authorizing my presence in the forth-coming shugyō. Sternly, the monk leads me inside and motions for me to strip my clothes off. I am given a pair of straw *waraji* sandals, a kind of knicker, deer pelt, under-kimono, hemp cloth over-robe, a conch shell in a net bag to wear over my shoulder, and a small black lacquered cap to wear over my forehead. Steadily the other new initiates arrive looking afraid and as bewildered as I feel. I am the only gaijin (foreigner) in the group.

In a smug way I am happy about this, yet a little nervous, with the language gap and cultural dissimilarities. There will be no sleep for me this first night, with my amped nerves and the frog-like croaks of those sleeping beside me on the tatami-covered floor.

I am disoriented in the morning as the croaks are replaced by the sound of mantras and the morning shuffles. Monks rise early. A conch shell blows the command to wake up and get dressed. Observing my fellow initiates, I learn what the commands mean. There will be no food or sleep for the next five days. I am fit and eager. My brain screams: *Bring it on, bring it all; I want this badly.*

Inside the temple, the priest, Sho-Daisendatsu, performs a ritual to transfer our souls into the Oi for protection. We chant the Heart Sutra and the *horagai* conch is blown to let the mountain spirits know we are on our way to the realm of the dead. The priest waves a long pole with white strips of paper at the top. One last blow of the conch and we are off. I finger my *nenju* rosary nervously. Walking through the town of Haguro-machi in our white Yama-bushi uniforms, as the township looks on in silent reverence, I am transported back to boot camp in the Navy. The geognosis of the Yamabushi gives them a special status in society and immunity from natural, and not so natural, threats from the mountains. Under my breath I hum a marching cadence and feel happy; I am so far away from everything and everyone. The cypress forest around the mountain smells ancient and mysterious.

"*Wa!*" Inside the gate to the mountain realm our group begins to run up the mountain's 2,446 stone steps. I feel wild and free, and the spirits are calling me forward. "Wa!" I scream over and over as I run up the mountain into the unknown. "Wa!" We pass a weather-beaten, five-story, 600-year-old, plain wooden pagoda. The path is flanked by stone lanterns. Halfway up the mountain, panting and out of breath, we stop at a small teahouse for a drink of water. There will only be water from here on out. "Wa!"

We stay constantly on the move, climbing, wading through streams, chanting in caves and meditating under waterfalls at sunrise. There is only water. Day one is manageable, days two and three hellish, and finally the bliss arrives on day four. I mean real, hot-damn-this-feels-good bliss. Who'd of thought starving oneself could lead to altered states of euphoria? Day and night we move through the sacred landscape of Dewa Sanzan, with Haguro, Gassan, and Yudono-san mountains our temple playground. Often we walk and climb vine-covered mountains for twelve straight hours before stopping for a rest. There is no sleep, only water. We build huge *Goma* fires deep in the forest, practice complex hand mudras and chant epic mantras. I begin to feel found and lost all at once. Initiates drop like flies, often simply wandering away, awash in the fairytale bath and hot meal down in the village. With their exit I grow stronger and wonder how far I can push this deprivation thing. On day four I begin to smell food miles away and see the landscape around me in a microspore kind of way.

I know that the Yamabushi come from the Shugendo sect; a combination of Buddhism, Shinto, Taoism and mysticism. They were the monks of Japanese lore—warriors, mountain ascetics— with supernatural powers like the folkloric character Tengu in Japanese drama. In a way, the Yamabushi are liminal beings that live between both worlds and have special access to knowledge to which normal humans cannot be privy. They are folk magicians, divinatory messengers and the overseers of demonic exorcism.

On day four, my warrior spirit begins to show itself and the forced marches become pleasurable and anticipated. On the morning of day five, we sit under a remote waterfall, with the water hitting our heads dead center, while the sun slowly makes its appearance. With my new-found night vision, the change from night to day becomes meaningless. I am hung over a cliff by my ankles. Then I am offered a red *umeboshi* salted plum. It will be the first food I have eaten in five days, and I hesitate before stuffing it into my mouth. "Wa!" My brain explodes with the taste, and I nearly fall to the ground. I am led to a small wooden building, with the eleven remaining initiates, to sleep. It is over, or so I think.

I feel deeply sick when the conch horn blows the command to wake up and get dressed. I have no watch or idea how long I have slept. We are served a bowl of miso soup and two rice-ball *onigiri*. I feel beyond hungry and could eat a tatami mat if it were served to me. We spend the entire day chanting mantras; I occasionally fall asleep and get wacked by the muscular monk who had initially given me my uniform. The toes I froze on Annapurna begin to cause me excruciating pain. I want to cry. At sunset we begin a round of full prostrations and there seems to be no end in sight. I quickly become drenched in my own sweat and the muscular monk seems to be purposely looming over me with his bamboo stick. I am sure he wants to torture me for some previous crime committed against him by a foreigner. My "Wa" becomes "Mu."

We are allowed outside to draw water. I wash my face and drink deeply. I look around at the other initiates and notice their weariness and dog-eared determination. I realize we are down to the core group. The conch horn blows and we quickly return to the small wooden building. The windows are being shuttered closed. Several monks bring charcoal barbeques into the room; something isn't right. Hadn't I read somewhere about a "smoking out" or *namban* session involving chili peppers? I go into survival mode and cover my face with my kimono sleeve, creating an air pocket, as I would in an avalanche. The ninjas arrive quickly, dressed in black. Chili peppers are thrown into the coals and a great cloud of smoke rises and expands across the room; the ninjas depart quickly and lock us in. I take a deep breath and go inward to wait it out. I hear horrific screams around me. Initiates are trying to escape and pounding on the doors. I drift into a dive memory; I am underwater and looking at tropical fish. Time becomes distorted and I seem to be swimming.

Fresh air assaults my face and exposed hands. The ritual is over, and the room looks like a war zone full of casualties. Many of the initiates are gagging and seem traumatized. I walk outside and look up at the stars, wondering what the next test will be. A large fire is built in the woods, and I am convinced we will be made to walk across hot coals. Fortunately, this isn't the case and we are simply taught how to properly build a ceremonial Goma fire and jump through it.

This is the beginning of our rebirth and entry back into the living realm. Yes, the more advanced Yamabushi can walk on fire. I am permanently in an altered state of being. At sunrise we sit under a waterfall, chanting the Heart Sutra.

For lunch we are served our first proper meal, with sake and a rest afterwards. The comfort seems odd and trick-like. Sure enough, just as I am dozing off into a deep sleep, the conch horn blows. Once assembled, we are told that we will be having a Tengu sumo wrestling tournament and the villagers are invited to come watch. What next?

I step out into the sand ring, wearing my *mawashi* loincloth, feeling like I am in a Fellini film. There is a group of local villagers watching. I hear women gasp when they see my tattoos; to them it is a sign that I belong to the Yakuza—Japanese mafia—which of course I do not. What the other initiates and monks don't know is that I was a state wrestling champion.

I lose one match out of ten and find myself in the championship round with the same man I had previously lost to. I have been told he has a black belt in judo. In the middle of the ring we crouch nose-to-nose waiting for the referee to drop the fan that signals the beginning of the match. One of us needs to throw the other outside of the circle. When our eyes meet, I begin to growl and bare my teeth; it is my animal spirit rising up. For a split second I see fear in his eyes. The match is over in a flash, and my opponent has no idea what hit him. He lies in a heap outside the ring, and I am the Yamabushi sumo champion of Dewa Sanzan. The highest priests must now wash my body in a sacred stream, and the initiates must each drink a cup of sake with me in honor. I am quickly drunk … and find myself witnessing an exorcism.

A middle-aged woman is lying on the ground and is surrounded by several of the priests from our group. I attempt to quietly hide behind a tree and watch (something tells me they know I am watching and want me to). I am drunk with sake and surrealism. There is a ring of candles around the woman's body, and I notice another woman dressed in black, holding the possessed woman's head in her hands. I wonder if she is a blind *miko*—the women who help remove evil spirits during exorcisms. Five priests are doing complicated finger and hand positions and chanting a haunting mantra. Suddenly, there seems to be a transfer of spirit between the two women, like a power surge. They both jerk about wildly and moan. I almost piss myself and quickly stagger away and back to our remote lodging, feeling half mad. Had I seen a fox, those malignant evil spirits in Japanese mythology? I feel so weak and alienated; I want to go home and forget this ever happened. I admit to myself that I have been spiritual shopping; I am not cut out for this soul-twisting upheaval. Again, the five-year-old boy that still dwells inside of me wants to cry and be hugged.

During the second week our initiation enters a new phase in

which ceremony and ritual are being transmitted to us while we move up streams and mountains, into remote forested valleys and in the caves where we often sleep.

Ritual for the Yamabushi is based on the needs of the parishioners and can include fortune telling, divination, prayers, incantations, spells and the creation of charms. We pay reverence to former Yamabushi through their skeleton bones, often left in the back recesses of the places where we sleep. I find this eerie and frightening in an innocent way. Monks often spend months alone in these remote caves, eating their mudras and drinking the mantras.

I grow tired of listening to the Japanese language and the competitive atmosphere that seems to be developing amongst the initiates. I feel their resentment because of the sumo victory and the benefits I have received as a result. I am very close to abandoning the Yamabushi journey and simply wandering across Japan alone, like an old-world *komusō* mendicant monk, seeking my own Way like the monk Ikkyu "Crazy Cloud."

One day we complete the entire Dewa Sanzan circuit of the three mountains—Haguro, Gassan and Yudono. I enjoy being up high in the wide-open spaces, breathing in the fresh air and feeling the sacredness of my surroundings. Hikers back off the path, gawking when I pass. It is one thing to see a Yamabushi—yet another to see a foreigner dressed in the traditional outfit of the mountain mystic. I do feel like I have gone from a death-like existence and come back alive during this initiation with the Yamabushi.

In a final ceremony I must come face-to-face with the head Yamabushi priest for a last interview.

"What you have learned, seen, experienced, is not to be shared with the outside world. Ring the bell and leave."

"Wa!" I run down the mountain as a Yamabushi.

Following my shugyō initiation I go on a week-long sake binge and fall backwards into the profane world from which I came. I am not ready for enlightenment yet. Or, as the travel writer Tim Cahill once said, "I'll pass on the enlightenment" for now.

"Woman with a stone fox at Yokkaichi" by Utagawa Kuniyoshi

IN THE GARDEN OF THE FOX

Anne Sigmon

Even in one single leaf on a tree, or in one blade of grass,
the awesome Deity presents itself.

—Shinto saying

My visit to Kyoto's famous Fushimi Inari shrine veered off track
even before I left the parking lot.

One of the oldest and most revered Shinto shrines in Japan,
Fushimi Inari was the one site I'd most wanted to explore in depth
as I traveled around Japan with a group of friends.

Fushimi is a UNESCO World Heritage site founded in 711 CE.
The shrine sits on a holy mountain, a shaded retreat with altars
dotted on a tangle of forested trails that snake up a seven-hundred-
sixty-four-foot peak. It is guarded, believers say, by magical foxes,
those tricky denizens of Japanese folklore.

I'd been feeling down in recent months and a bit scared. Health problems stemming from a stroke and autoimmune disease, which had been under control for over a decade, had started to roar like demons again. For the first time in years, I felt uneasy about the future. I needed a physical and psychic reboot. Surely experiencing the mystery of Shinto—with its reverence for nature and spiritual connection—would be a balm for my worries.

Fushimi Inari would be the perfect place to explore Shinto, a spiritual practice as old as the Japanese people. Shinto, which means the "way of the gods," has no set dogma. Rather, it emphasizes sincerity and harmony with nature. It is a contemplative faith that inspires a sense of wonder in the beholder. I was more than ready for that!

But today's visit wouldn't be easy on my creaky, arthritic knees, damaged by too many autoimmune skirmishes. The five-mile walk up the mountain and back included a seven-hundred-fifty-foot elevation gain and twelve thousand steps. My guidebook suggested two to three hours for the excursion.

My friends and I had planned to take the train from Tokyo to Kyoto, have lunch and a guided tour of the National Museum and a leisurely late-afternoon sojourn at the Inari shrine. But the National Museum tour had been pushed to the end of the day by our hosts; we would need to visit Fushimi Inari first.

We arrived at about 1:30 p.m., dashing by taxi straight from the Tokyo train.

"We'll see the site on our own," our trip coordinator announced as soon as we pulled into the parking area of the shrine. "But I need you back here in an hour and twenty minutes." She tapped her watch for emphasis. "We'll go for a late lunch, then to the National Museum for our 4:30 tour. Don't be late."

My friends hustled off at a trot, determined to rush to the top and back. I just stood in the parking lot, shaking my head, shoulders tight, stifling frustration. Introspection on a stopwatch? *Really?* Then a thought landed like a feather: *Follow your own path.*

A weight seemed to lift when I told the trip leader not to expect me for lunch. "I'll make my own way and meet the group at the museum." Relieved to have more time to explore, I relaxed, breathing in the citrus-y aroma of the cedar forest and the incense sold from vendor booths near the entrance.

Several enormous vermilion torii (shrine gates) marked the entrance to the site, followed by an elaborate gatehouse called the *rōmon* gate, among the tallest in all Japan. Behind the gatehouse was a confusing constellation of traditional Japanese hip-roofed buildings framed in bright red with gleaming golden decorations. The main temple (*honden*), built in 1499, was flanked by two large stone foxes wearing red cloth bibs. I watched from a respectful distance as an elderly couple stood in front of what I assumed was an altar, saying prayers and bowing. But it was hardly a reverent experience. The early September day was mild, but overcast and humid. All around me, hectic and rushed crowds of tourists babbled and laughed, then set off huffing up the mountain—some in kimono, others in jeans and sweat-soaked shirts weighted down with daypacks.

Fushimi Inari is world famous for its thousands of flame-colored torii gates—the Senbon Torii—that form an eerie tunnel winding up the mountainside. Torii represent the passage from the worldly to the sacred. The orange-red color, originally made from cinnabar, is called *shuiro* in Japanese, representing the color of the sun. I imagined them as a path leading from the present to the past, from the living to the spirit world.

The Shinto faith believes in kami, the divine power found in all things. Kami may be gods, spirits, supernatural forces and even ancestors. Kami gravitate to the natural beauty found around mountains, waterfalls, trees and unusually shaped rocks. That's why Shinto shrines are found in such numinous spaces. There are virtually an unlimited number of Shinto kami. Many individuals and families venerate their own personal spirits. But there is a pantheon of about fifteen major gods. One of the most popular is Inari Ōkami, the god of rice and the harvest—now expanded to include business and trade. Fushimi is the head Inari shrine in all Japan; there are many thousands of others across the country.

Shinto gods have "messengers." Inari's is the white fox or *kitsune*, which is seen as a sacred and mysterious creature. At almost every turn at Fushimi, I saw statues of foxes, usually in pairs, most of them seated.

From the temple complex, I moved on to the phalanx of magnificent torii, many of them fifteen or twenty feet tall. The tunnel of gates rose through an ever-changing forest of pine, cedar, cypress and maple. There were cherry trees, ferns and even bamboo. Leaves rustled like the mountain's breath. I had imagined that the trip through those stunning gates would be magical, a mystical voyage to the spirit world. But there didn't seem to be any room for magic or mystery that day, just a horde of sweating tourists, packed elbow to elbow, wielding umbrellas and four-foot selfie sticks like samurai swords. This was the right place for Shinto reverence, but without the peace.

At several spots up the slope, the gates opened into small plazas with red-painted shrines. Racks displayed horoscopes and wooden prayer cards (called *ema*) shaped like fox heads.

Feeling sticky in the heat, I sat on a bench to rest with my camera in hand, hoping for just a tiny break in the solid wall of people. I hoped to snatch one of those iconic shots of the torii tunnel—sans tourists. *Futile*, I sighed after about ten minutes. Discouraged, I stepped back into the tunnel. The clock was ticking as I sweated and climbed, dodging backpacks and tripods and selfie sticks. Did I really want to spend my remaining time in this crowd?

Just then, I noticed a hint of a trail leading downhill away from the madness. At a break in the gates, I stepped out and followed the curving path through the woods. Before long, I saw a single torii, weathered to bare wood, long past any shade of vermilion. Beyond it, in a shady glen, what looked like a gated cottage stood surrounded by lovingly cared-for plantings. But this was no cottage; it was a small shrine with two scarlet torii of a more human size. The gates led to an altar with a kneeling bench in front of an offering chest. Behind it, a half-flight of weathered stone stairs led to a walkway and on to what looked like an enchanted garden of stone. I was alone.

In that square space of perhaps an eighth of an acre, hundreds of incised and artfully-placed stones perched atop walls, about four feet tall, built of tightly-fitted boulders. Most of the stones were covered with moss. Each one bore an inscription of deeply-carved and painted Japanese kanji characters, a style popular a century ago. The script was indecipherable to me, yet it spoke of a reverence that required no words. Miniature torii stood in front of some of the stones, ceramic votives before others. The place seemed lovingly but not recently tended. A stone Inari fox stood guard in a back corner. It wore a tattered cloth bib of long-faded red and in its mouth held a gem signifying its power to grant wishes. Its mate— these foxes usually come in pairs—was missing.

The rocks resembled the kind of ancient standing stones I'd once seen in Cornwall. Some were as tall as giants, others as small as children. They looked like a chorus of hooded ghosts. I imagined they might be gravestones. The place smelled of moss, damp earth and great age. Tall trees and stout bushes surrounded it. Through the breaks in the foliage, weak light shone from behind the clouds. The silence was broken only by the whine of cicadas and the breeze through the cypress trees.

But what were these stones? How old were they? I didn't know. I didn't speak the language; I didn't have a guide. This corner of the mountain was uncharted in any of the articles or guidebooks I'd seen. Even though I couldn't understand any of the characters, the spirit of this place touched me. I felt like I had passed through the torii gates to a land beyond.

I wandered, alone, from stone to stone, feeling the cool rock, brushing my hand against the moss, trying to imagine who was honored here. But the question that kept popping up for me was time. How best to spend my time. No doctor could tell me how much time I had left in this world or whether my illness would rob me of the time I thought should be my due. Most days I tried my best to live a "normal" life filled with work and chores, friends and family, books and travel—trying, like everyone else, to balance it all. But there were days, more numerous now, when I feared I was missing some great existential point. What did I gain by trying to be "normal" when I'm not? A woman with stroke deficits, mental confusion and autoimmune disease can't carry a "normal" load. Is normal the objective? Or should it be something with deeper meaning?

My time for the day was up. The clouds turned dark. The mist turned to rain. I had no idea where I was on the mountain or how to get back down to the entrance, where I'd need to find a taxi to take me to the museum to meet my friends. That kind of confusion sometimes worried me, but on that day, I found my way down with ease, buoyed by the peace I'd found in the garden.

At one of the plazas down the hill, I studied a billboard map of the park. I wanted to pinpoint the place that had touched me. I saw many shrines and waystations highlighted on the map, but no magical garden of stones. Instead, in the place where I thought I'd been, the map showed a drawing of heavy white clouds in the shape of a fox—the only such spot on the mountain.

I rejoined my friends and enjoyed the rest of our sojourn in Japan. The mystery of Shinto did not touch me in the phalanx of ten thousand red torii, as I'd hoped, and I never reached the top of the holy mountain. Instead, I found magic by wandering—lost, confused and on my own path—into a mystical garden of stone. I never learned who was honored there or how long the stones had rested in that holy place. In the end, that didn't matter. What remained was the sense of reverence.

It occurred to me that, even in the absence of a common history or language, those ancestors had a lesson to teach me. When we take the time to relax and listen, the spirits of holy places like Fushimi Inari call to us, inviting us to listen to our hearts, to heed the lessons that are already deep within us.

They whispered to me that day in that garden of the fox: *Your time to make a difference is now.*

Visitors at Meiji Jingu

Moment at Meiji Jingu

Lowry McFerrin

I had traveled to Japan many times for work, although it was always a stepping-stone to other Asian destinations like Hong Kong, Singapore or Kuala Lumpur. Truth be told, I hadn't really been to Japan at all. Airports are not the way to experience a city, much less a country.

That changed when our nephew, Peter, responded positively to our offer to take him anywhere in the world he wanted to go after graduating from high school. His sister, Eileen, chose Paris for her graduation trip. Peter chose Tokyo.

Linda, my wife, lived in Japan for several years as a girl, then later visited occasionally as a novelist and while on assignment as a travel writer. So, when Peter made his Tokyo graduation trip choice, she set out to create a terrific adventure for him. Little did I know that this trip wasn't designed just for Peter. It was also arranged for me. Her itinerary offered many once-in-a-lifetime experiences and one unexpected life-changing event.

One such experience was dining at the top of the Park Hyatt Tokyo in Shinjuku, where the gallery-like entrance to the 40th-floor restaurant, Kozue, displayed spot-lit examples of Chef Kenichiro

Ooe's personal collection of masterfully crafted ceramic ware. Once inside the restaurant, we were greeted with impeccable service by a welcoming team of servers and a large ice-filled bowl of varying sake cups. We each chose one cup from the bowl to drink from during our multi-course kaiseki meal, as a different sake was paired and poured with each locally sourced dish and delicacy. Yep, once in a lifetime....

Another such experience was a VIP invitation to a big bash atop the Grand Hyatt Tokyo, commemorating the opening of Roppongi Hills and celebrating noted Japanese artist, Takashi Murakami, sometimes referred to as Japan's Andy Warhol because of his "Superflat" theory, his contributions to the fashion world, his Pop Art style and his popularity. Murakami's fanciful designs and characters were incorporated into offerings from Louis Vuitton and other brands for international distribution. They were also being featured at the Grand Hyatt Tokyo.

We were escorted directly to Murukami and afforded an opportunity to personally congratulate him on his successes. Prior to that introduction, however, we had a short visit with Mr. Minoru Mori, event sponsor and one of the most influential financiers in Tokyo. This, the spectacular Roppongi Hills project—tower, complex and museum—owed its existence to him. We were followed by dozens of photographers as we bowed and shook his hand. As unknowns, we mystified the paparazzi, who were curious about our identities yet remained respectfully distant as we were ushered through the crowds. We couldn't really mingle, but we had a great time enjoying the scene. Then we were escorted to the helipad on top of the building. Yep, another once-in-a-lifetime experience.

Thanks to Linda, our week-long Tokyo visit included many such experiences, but there is one event that stands out above the others.

The plan was to take the subway to Meiji-jingu, one of the largest and most dramatic Shinto shrines in Tokyo. It was a warm, humid and windless afternoon. It seemed to me that the train ride took a long time—maybe 45 minutes. That was ok, though, because this was a very personal trip for Linda, as she wanted to honor her mother, Genie, who had recently passed away, with a traditional Shinto ritual—ringing the temple bell, making an offering, clapping her hands, bowing, praying quietly and bowing again.

The expansive grounds beckoned as Peter and I followed Linda through the shrine's massive torii gate. At first, we were going to join her at the interior temple steps and witness, close-hand, the ritual Linda was to perform. However, I held back, mentioning to Peter that Linda should do this alone, or as alone as possible, since there'd probably be lots of people walking in and around the main shrine. So, we both stood by the gate and watched Linda reverently cross the courtyard, cleanse hands and mouth at a wooden washing station, and approach the main hall.

What was uncanny was the area in front of the main hall ... there was no one there. This was odd as it was in the middle of the afternoon and there were usually crowds of people everywhere we went, especially at a popular tourist stop like the grandest Shinto shrine in Tokyo. Amazed at the stillness, we watched and waited....

As Linda approached the main hall, a sudden gust of wind started swirling around her, lifting gently her skirt and tossing small dust clouds at her feet. We felt nothing but the still, humid heat of the day. It was as if the wind was only there for Linda, swirling around her, accompanying her to the temple steps. I suddenly had the sense that Genie had joined Linda on her spiritual trek across the grounds, right up to the main altar. Her gusty companion continued to swirl around her as she prayed and reverently bowed once … twice … three times.

Peter and I looked at one another in awe as chills ran up and down our bodies.

Then, as suddenly as it came, the wind stopped. As quiet as the place was when we arrived, it was noisy, filled with dozens of people walking around the grounds, checking out the shrine, the out-buildings, the bell. After Linda's ritual, which the Shinto spirits obviously blessed, the shrine became a tourist attraction again.

Linda walked slowly back to where we were standing. We excitedly shared our observations and exhilaration with her. She smiled and acknowledged that she felt Genie's blessing and her ancestors' presence. We had witnessed a beautiful and bold moment … an event. It wasn't planned. It wasn't expected. It was personal. It was transformative.

This was Japan.

A magical Japanese badger, or *tanuki*

GLOSSARY

amae	concept of love and dependency at the root of Japanese relationships
arigato	thank you
chabudai	low table
chindogu	ingenious gadgets that may cause more problems than they solve (literally, "weird tools")
chirashi	big bowl of rice mixed with fish and vegetables (literally, "scattered")
depachika	basement-level food courts in Japanese department stores
ema	wooden prayer cards
geiko	word for *geisha* in the Kyoto dialect
Goma	ritual Buddhist ceremonial fires
hai	yes

haiden	hall of worship
hamon	Japanese slit drum
hanami	custom of viewing cherry blossoms in full bloom
henshin	practice in which tourists are transformed into ersatz geisha
honden	sanctuary where Japanese folk deities (kami) reside
horagai	large conch shell used as a trumpet
Inari Ōkami	Japanese god of rice and the harvest—now expanded to include business and trade
jinja	Shinto shrine
jisei	centuries-old Japanese tradition of death poems
kakefuton	comforter similar to a duvet
kanzashi	ornaments used in traditional Japanese hairstyles
katsuobushi	smoked bonito fish
katsura	traditional elaborate Japanese wig
kawaii	cuteness culture
kitsune	in Japanese folklore, spirit foxes with paranormal abilities

kodoku	loneliness, sadness, isolation
kombu	dried kelp
komusō	Japanese mendicant monks
kotatsu	heating table covered by a quilt
kyukei	"short stay" in a Love Hotel
machiga	error, blunder or indiscretion
machiya	traditional wooden townhouse
maiko	an apprentice geisha
maneki-neko	good fortune cats
mawashi	loincloth worn by sumo wrestlers during training or competition
miko	Shinto shrine maiden (literally, "child of God")
mu	a concept meaning "without" or "nothing"
nanban	spicy red peppers
nanban ibushi	devotional practice of sitting in a room with braziers of burning chili peppers
nenju	prayer beads
nigiri-sushi	sushi made of a hand-pressed rice oval topped with raw fish
nomiya	tiny bar or saloon

obake	shape-shifting creatures of Japanese folklore
O'Bon	Japanese Buddhist Festival of the Dead
ofuro	short, steep-sided wooden bathtub
okiya	lodging house with which a maiko or geisha is affiliated during her career
okobo	traditional wooden platform sandals worn by apprentice geisha
okonomiyaki	Japanese pizza (*yaki* translates to "grilled" and *okonomi* means "as you like")
omakase	Japanese tradition of asking the chef to select your order
oni	cruel and malicious demonic creature of Japanese folklore
onigiri	rice balls, often wrapped in nori
oshiroi	white foundation used by kabuki actors, geisha and maiko
ozen	low tray-table
Pocari Sweat	popular beverage designed to replace water and electrolytes
rōmon gate	two-story gatehouse at a Shinto shrine
ryokan	traditional Japanese inn
sakkō	hairstyle worn by maiko

sakura	flowering cherry tree; cherry blossoms
sembei	crackers in seaweed wrappers
senbon torii	red torii gates sheltering a long pathway
sentachi	novice Yamabushi monk
shakyo	meditative practice of hand writing sutras over and over
Shinkansen	Japanese bullet train
shogin ryori	restrained Buddhist devotional cuisine
shoryodana	altar to welcome ancestors and spirits in the O'Bon Festival
shugyō	austere, deep mind-body training
shuiro	vermilion or scarlet color
shukubo	pilgrims' lodgings
sudare	traditional Japanese screens or blinds
tokonoma	alcove used for display
umeboshi	salty pickled Japanese plum
wa	a cultural concept meaning something like "harmony"
wabi-sabi	Japanese aesthetic concept that appreciates simplicity, imperfection and transience
waraji	light, tie-on sandals, usually made of straw

washoku	traditional Japanese cuisine that grows from a respect for nature, harmony, beauty and nutrition
Yamabushi	ascetic mountain hermit monks
yukata	summer kimono
zabuton	floor cushions that make sitting or kneeling more comfortable
zaru soba	chilled buckwheat noodles served with dipping sauce

Previous Publications and Awards

"Spooky, Spooky Tokyo" by Linda Watanabe McFerrin is excerpted from an article published in the *San Francisco Chronicle Magazine* in 2000.

"Bowing to Washoku" by Anne Sigmon won a gold Solas Award from Travelers' Tales in 2020.

A version of "The Way of Wagyu" by Laurie McAndish King was published as "The Secret of Kobe Beef" by BATW Travel Stories on Medium.com in April, 2022.

"Containment" and "In Tokyo, Finding the Kami Way" by Linda Watanabe McFerrin were published in the author's award-winning collection *Navigating the Divide* (Alan Squire Publishing, 2019).

"Nun for a Day: Wandering in Koyasan" by MJ Pramik earned an honorable mention from Solas Awards in 2017.

"Okonomiyaki" by Laurie McAndish King was published in the author's award-winning collection *An Elephant Ate My Arm: More True Stories from a Curious Traveler* (Destination Insights, 2021).

"Echoes of Okunoin" won a gold Solas Award from Travelers' Tales in 2018 and was published as a single-story e-book by Hidden Compass.

"Whirling and Swirling Along the Way" by Rob "Tor" Torkildson was excerpted from *The Walkabout Chronicles: Epic Journeys by Foot* (2016).

Author Biographies

Daphne Beyers grew up near Amish country in northeastern Pennsylvania, often finding herself caught in traffic behind wheel and buggy carriages. She's lived in many places, including London, New York City, San Francisco, Berkeley, and Palm Springs. Daphne taught herself to program at the age of thirteen and works as a computer consultant for various Fortune 500 companies. Her first essay, "Existential Cafe," was published in an award-winning anthology of Parisian stories, *Wandering in Paris: Luminaries and Love in the City of Light.*

Daphne's essays have also appeared in *Wandering in Cornwall: Mystery, Mirth and Transformation in the Land of Ancient Celts, Wandering in Andalusia: The Soul of Southern Spain* and *Wandering in Greece: Athens, Islands and Antiquities.* Daphne currently lives in South Carolina with two Scottish terriers, Bhava and Haiku.

Joanna Biggar is a teacher, writer and traveler whose special places of the heart include the California coast and the South of France. As a professional writer for thirty years, she has written poetry, fiction, personal essays, features, news and travel articles for hundreds of publications including the *Washington Post Magazine,*

Psychology Today, the *International Herald Tribune,* and the *Wall Street Journal.* Her most recent travel essays have appeared in the *Wandering* series, whose anthologies include books on Costa Rica, Bali, Paris, Cornwall, Andalusia, Cuba, and Greece. *That Paris Year,* the first in her trilogy of novels, was published by Alan Squire Publishing in 2010, followed by *Melanie's Song* in 2019. She has taught journalism, creative writing, personal essay and travel writing in many venues, and has juried the annual awards for the Northern California chapter of the Society of Professional Journalists. She serves on the Board of Directors of Emiliano Zapata Street Academy in Oakland, California, where she makes her home, and is a longtime member of the Society of Woman Geographers.

Mary Brent Cantarutti, born, bred and reared to be a fan-carrying lady, headed west in pursuit of romance and adventure. She never lost her drawl. Co-founder of the Southern Sampler Artists Colony and writer of Southern women's fiction, her inner compass points toward cooling Atlantic breezes.

Her first book, the popular *A Child's Marin,* highlighted family destinations in Northern California's small but beautiful Marin County (the one sandwiched between San Francisco and the Wine Country). She also updated the Marin and North Coast sections of *Best Places Northern California* (4th edition, Sasquatch Books).

The Bottle Tree, her first novel (originally titled *Kudzu Rising*), was a finalist in the Novel-in-Progress category of the 2010 William Faulkner-William Wisdom Creative Writing Competition, and also a finalist in the Novel category in 2011. Mary Brent lives with her husband, Lido Cantarutti, and a fuzzy-orange cat, Mandarino, in San Rafael, California.

Thomas Harrell has joined the ranks of former lawyers turned writers. Since a chronic health condition forced him to leave the active practice of law, he has turned lemons into lemonade by writing fiction instead of briefs (some might say they are not too dissimilar) and travel essays. His writing, both personal and travel-related, often involves history, which he has always loved. Tom most enjoys writing short stories and essays, but like so many writers dreams of completing a novel, most likely some improbable mash-up of history, fantasy, philosophy and humor, leavened with enough erotica to keep the pages turning.

His *Wandering* anthology stories reflect special travel destinations steeped in history and culture, the diverse enthusiasms and encouragement of his fellow writers, and the "aha" moments that inspire every writer and come if you wander enough.

Lenny Karpman writes from his *finca* and refuge for birds and animals in Costa Rica's Central Valley. He has authored thirteen books, several dozen articles, editorials, opinion pieces and reviews in magazines, newspapers and anthologies. His usual subjects are food, travel, civil liberties and human rights. He apprenticed at a French restaurant in San Francisco, practiced cardiology for more than thirty years and served on the boards and legislative policy committees for three large non-profits. He was editor of *San Francisco Medicine* and director of Northern California Kaiser Permanente's regional Cardiac Catheterization Laboratory. Lenny shares his life, happiness and wanderlust with his wife, Joan Hall, JD. They have three adult children and seven grandchildren.

Lowry McFerrin's interest in letters began at a very early age. He wanted to be a high school English teacher. During his early student years, he practiced journalism—first as the Sports Editor of his high school newspaper, *Tam News*, then as a reporter for the *College of Marin Times*.

After graduating from SFSU, however, he chose to work in the family business, a commercial print company in San Francisco's Montgomery Street district. This background eventually led him to a position as Vice President, International Sales & Marketing for a privately held barcode label manufacturer and a member of its board of directors. Throughout this period he wrote many trade articles for the Auto ID industry but, as a poet at heart, he balanced that type of writing with literary work.

Today, Lowry offers and counsels on therapeutic massage at medical, health and fitness centers as well as at his own Oakland, California, studio. A tai chi instructor and an avid traveler and fiddle player, he has worked with and entertained people around the world, occasionally focusing his energy on travel essays and poetry.

Ethel Mussen is a doughty centenarian who lives high on a hill above Berkeley and enjoys the wide-eyed enthusiasm of the Wanderland travelers as they hunker down in off-beat places to explore the world. Fifty years in providing health care of various sorts—the last 35 in teaching about and treating speech and hearing disorders—honed her anthropological approach to people and customs. A collector's interest in potters and their ceramics offered an additional slant in the production and business of local craftsmen. Repeated spells of living in New Zealand, France and Italy gave more insight into the effects and variety of cultural assumptions in local politics, business and behavior. These experiences and interests bias Ethel's emotional and scholarly response to the beauty and strangeness of each new voyage. With every discovery, good or bad, her late husband, Paul, used to regale her and their two children with the assurance that "This is a cultural experience!" She utters that mantra with each new trip.

Mary Jean (MJ) Pramik, a coalminer's daughter and great grand-daughter of the Mongolian plain, survived the COVID-19 pandemic without howling. As a trained molecular biologist and vaccine researcher, MJ followed the intrigues of the viral attack with piqued interest. Pre-pandemic, she published in medical journals and mainstream publications such as *Good Housekeeping* and the *National Enquirer*. She has contributed to the Travelers' Tales *Venturing* series on the Canal du Midi and Southern Greece, and *Wandering* anthologies on Costa Rica, Bali, Cornwall, Andalusia, Cuba and Greece, for which she's won several Solas Awards. MJ blogs about travel and environment at "Travel in Times of Catastrophic Change." She's completed her first novel, *COAL*, and a collection of poetry. Her poem, "Rocks, Stones," was nominated for a Pushcart Prize.

Michele Rivers is a renaissance woman. She celebrates life as an artist, author, a C.P.I.T.S. poetry teacher and interior designer. She is the author of *Time for Tea: Tea and Conversations with Thirteen English Women* and produced and hosted *Time for Tea*, a six-part television series for Channel 26 TV. Michele's English accent could also be heard on KWMR 90.5 FM, where her *Time for Tea* interview radio show aired for several years. Michele's artwork has been exhibited at Commonweal, California Pacific Medical Center and the Atrium Gallery at Marin Oncology. Her driftwood sculptures and altars have been selected for exhibition at the International Rumi Conference at the Robert J. Fullerton Art Museum. Michele has been the recipient of grants for *Creating Sacred Space* by the Lloyd Symington Foundation and the Mental Insight Foundation. Michele lives in Marin County, California, where the landscape reminds her of her homeland in the English countryside.

Tania Amochaev Romanov is the author of *Mother Tongue: A Saga of Three Generations of Balkan Women* (Travelers' Tales, 2018), also published in Serbian as *Po Našemu* (Akademis Kaknjiga, 2020); *Never a Stranger* (Solificatio, 2019), a collection of award-winning travel essays; and *One Hundred Years of Exile: A Romanov's Search for Her Father's Russia* (Travelers' Tales, 2020), published in Russia as *СТО ЛЕТ ИЗГНАНИЯ* (Rosspen Publishers, 2021) and winner of gold for memoir in the 27th annual Northern California Publishers and Authors Book Awards. Also a Solas Award winner, Tania's work has been featured in multiple travel anthologies, including *The Best Travel Writing* and *The Best Women's Travel Writing* series.

Born in the former Yugoslavia, Tania spent her childhood in a refugee camp in Italy before emigrating to the United States, where she grew up in San Francisco's Russian community. A graduate of San Francisco public schools, she went on to serve as CEO of three technology companies.

Anne Sigmon washed out of high school and college PE. After college, she headed for San Francisco and a communications career. Exotic travel was the stuff of dreams until, at 38, she married Jack, took tea with erstwhile headhunters in Borneo and climbed Mt. Kilimanjaro at 43. Five years later, she was zapped by a career-ending stroke caused by an obscure autoimmune disease called Antiphospholipid Syndrome (APS). She may be stuck with blood thinners and a damaged brain, but she's still traveling to the wild from Botswana to Syria, Iran and Uzbekistan.

Anne's essays and award-winning travel stories have appeared in national publications including *Good Housekeeping* and *Stroke Connection* magazines and the American Heart Association website. Her work has appeared in BestTravelWriting.com, *Wanderlust and Lipstick* and GeoEx.com digital magazines, and in a dozen anthologies, most recently Bradt Guide's *To Oldly Go* and *The Best Women's Travel Writing, Volume 12.*

Rob "Tor" Torkildson is a peripatetic traveler and lifelong seeker and explorer who has worked and lived around the world for the last 30 years. Torkildson has tramped through the Amazon, over the Himalaya, and across the Sahara in his quest to experience sacred landscapes in over 120 countries. He has worked as a diver, commercial fisherman, ship navigator, customs and immigration expert, writer and publisher, a fixer in Africa, and as a vintner and owner of the Wild Hare Winery in Sant'Alfio, Sicily. Torkildson has published three travel memoirs, a novella, and in such magazines as the *Kyoto Journal, Beat Scene, Ripcord Adventure Journal, Canadian Mountain Journal* and the *American Alpine Journal,* and has won two gold Solas Awards from Travelers' Tales. Torkildson has degrees in Asian history, psychology and a certificate in communication arts. He is an International Fellow of the Explorers Club, speaker for the Explorers Bureau, has carried the Explorers Museum pennant on expedition, and is a member of the Midgard Expedition led by Bjorn Heyerdahl.

EDITOR BIOGRAPHIES

Laurie McAndish King (LaurieKing.com) writes about seeing 20-foot-long Australian earthworms, walking on a man-eating lake, and learning from an Ivy League astrophysicist about how flying saucers are powered—not your typical travel writing. That's probably why *Kirkus Reviews* hails her as "an author with an eye for the quirky."

Laurie's award-winning stories and photography have appeared in *Smithsonian* magazine, the *San Francisco Chronicle*, *The Best Women's Travel Writing*, and other magazines and literary anthologies. A story in her first book, *Lost, Kidnapped, Eaten Alive*, earned the Lowell Thomas Gold Award for Cultural Travel. Her most recent book, *An Elephant Ate My Arm: More True Stories from a Curious Traveler*, won first place in the 2021 Paris Book Festival.

Laurie also wrote *An Erotic Alphabet* (for which she was dubbed "The Shel Silverstein of Erotica") and co-edited two books in the *Hot Flashes: sexy little stories & poems* series.

She is a member of Left Coast Writers, a past president of Bay Area Travel Writers, and a judge for the Northern California chapter of the Society of Professional Journalists' Excellence in Journalism awards. Laurie has an undergraduate degree in philosophy and a master's degree in education, and lives in northern California.

Linda Watanabe McFerrin
(www.lwmcferrin.com) is a poet, travel writer, novelist and contributor to numerous newspapers, magazines and anthologies. She is the author of two poetry collections, past editor of a popular Northern California guidebook and a winner of the Katherine Anne Porter Prize for Fiction. Her award-winning book-length fiction titles include *Namako: Sea Cucumber, The Hand of Buddha* and *Dead Love* (Stone Bridge Press, 2009), a Bram Stoker Award Finalist for Superior Achievement in a Novel.

In addition, Linda has co-edited fourteen anthologies, including the *Hot Flashes: sexy little stories & poems series*; judged the San Francisco Literary Awards, the Josephine Miles Award for Literary Excellence and the Kiriyama Prize; served as a visiting mentor for the Loft Mentor Series; and been guest faculty at the Oklahoma Arts Institute. A past NEA Panelist and juror for the Marin Literary Arts Council and the founder of Left Coast Writers®, she has led workshops in Greece, France, Italy, England, Ireland, Central America, Indonesia, Scotland, Spain, Japan and the United States and has mentored a long list of accomplished writers and best-selling authors toward publication. Her most recent book, *Navigating the Divide* (Alan Squire Publishing, 2019) was a Next Generation Indie Book Awards Finalist.